Luas – Harcourt Street Memories

LUAS
Harcourt Street Memories

BRIAN Mac AONGUSA

CURRACH
PRESS

First published in 2004 by
CURRACH PRESS
55a Spruce Avenue, Stillorgan Industrial Park, Blackrock, Co Dublin
www.currach.ie

Cover designed by Currach Press
Design concept by Susan Waine

Front cover: Luas tram in front of the old Harcourt Street Station © Railway Procurement Agency
Back cover: Steam train arriving at Rathmines & Ranelagh Station in 1955 © Barry Carse
Half-title page: Luas tram on Harcourt Street, © *The Irish Times* (Cyril Byrne)
Frontispiece: Luas tram crossing the Nine Arches at Milltown, © *The Irish Times* (Matt Kavanagh)

Origination by Currach Press
Printed in Ireland by Betaprint Ltd, Dublin

ISBN 1-85607-917-1

ACKNOWLEDGEMENTS

The author and publisher gratefully acknowledge the permission of the following to use photographic material and illustrations in their copyright:
Camera Press: p.95 (Samuel Beckett); Barry Carse: pp.63, 67 (right), 69, 87 (left) and 102; Gerry Donnelly: pp.64, 89, 118 and 122; Jim Dowling: pp.34, 36 (both), 84, 128, 133; Dublin Transportation Office: pp.29 and 31; Clifton Flewitt: p.18 (lower); Irish Railway Record Society: pp.39, 80, 91, 114, 127; *The Irish Times*: for the maps on pp.6 and 7 and photographs on the half-title page, frontispiece and on pp.14, 16 (lower), 19, 20, 26, 51 (Myles na Gopaleen); Seán Kennedy: pp.77 (lower), 81 (upper), 106, 108-109, 110, 113 and 116; Ultan Kennedy: p.96 (upper); Lensmen: pp.44 (C.S. Andrews) and 51 (Brendan Behan); Charles Meredith pp.35, 101; David Murray: p.88; National Library of Ireland: pp.38 (both O'Dea: 13/1 – upper and 5/88 – lower), 40, 42, 48, 57 (ref. O'Dea 2/91), 62 (ref. Eason 1718), 78 (ref. Morgan 130), 81 (lower), 100 (ref. Cardall 969); A. T. Newham p.98; Colm O'Callaghan: p.66; and the Railway Procurement Agency: pp.viii, 4, 8, 11, 12, 13, 15, 16 (upper), 18 (upper), 20, 23, 33, 134 and 135.

The author and publisher also wish to acknowledge the permission of the following to use material in their copyright:
Calder Publications for quotations from *Watt* and *Texts for Nothing* by Samuel Beckett;
and Faber & Faber for quotations from *All That Fall* and *That Time* by Samuel Beckett.

The range of illustrations in this book from the author's collection has been greatly enhanced by photographs and other material provided by the above, to whom the author is deeply indebted. Without their generous co-operation, this book would be much the poorer.

Every effort has been made to trace copyright holders. If we have inadvertently used copyright material without permission we apologise and will put it right in future editions.

Contents

Buíochas

vii

Preface

1

1. Luas a Reality

3

2. Reopening the Old Railway

10

3. Slow Awakening

24

4. Harcourt Street Line Closure

34

5. Why Did They Close It?

43

6. 'Sea Breeze' Excursions

59

7. Trains and Travellers

65

8. Character of the Old Line

83

9. The Drumm Trains

106

10. Accidents

112

Outline History of Harcourt Street Line

119

Appendices

127

Select Bibliography

136

To all those who devoted their considerable talents to building an elegant Luas system on the shoulders of The Harcourt Street Line.

BUÍOCHAS

This book could not have been produced to such a high standard without the generous co-operation of many people. The Chief Executive of the Railway Procurement Agency (RPA), Frank Allen, has been most supportive throughout, in providing me with full information on the development of Luas and facilitating my enquiries among his senior staff. The Chief Architect Jim Quinlan, Senior Architect Neil O'Brien and Public Relations Manager Tom Manning have all been most generous with their time in assisting me. Special thanks must go to Neil O'Brien for taking very fine photographs of Luas and generously providing copies of a selection of these to grace the cover and pages of this book.

Photographs and memories of the Harcourt Street Line have been assembled with the kind co-operation of many people. Jim Dowling provided great help with pictures, tickets and anecdotal information, while the renowned professional photographer Seán Kennedy was most generous in supplying many unique photographs, including those of the two major accidents in 1900 and 1957. Other fine photographs were made available by David Murray, Barry Carse, Colm O'Callaghan, Ultan Kennedy, Clifton Flewitt, Gerry Donnelly and Charles Meredith. The Honorary Archivist of the Irish Railway Record Society, Brendan Pender, went to considerable trouble also to locate rare photographs of trains on the Harcourt Street Line. Credit for bringing many of these to a very high standard must go to Janet Gillanders who achieved wonders from very old negatives.

I am especially indebted to Barry Carse for carefully checking my account of the considerable work carried out both by CIÉ and the RPA in the long process involved in the reopening of the Harcourt Street Line. I am also greatly indebted to many who agreed to speak to me at length about their memories of the old line, especially Jim Kiernan, Kathleen Delap, Dick Flynn, Carmel Rogan, Éamonn Doyle and Seán Ó Cinnéide, who also provided the unique photograph of his old colleagues taken by the late Alan T. Newham.

My most grateful thanks must again go to Seán O Boyle and Brian Lynch of The Columba Press and Currach Press, who courageously published my first book *The Harcourt Street Line : Back on Track* a year ago and encouraged me to put pen to paper once more for this second book. Neither book would have been so attractive without their professional help nor would they be as readable without the wise counsel of my loving wife, Máire Mac Aongusa.

Mo bhuíochas ó chroí díbh uilig.

BRIAN Mac AONGUSA
Samhain 2004

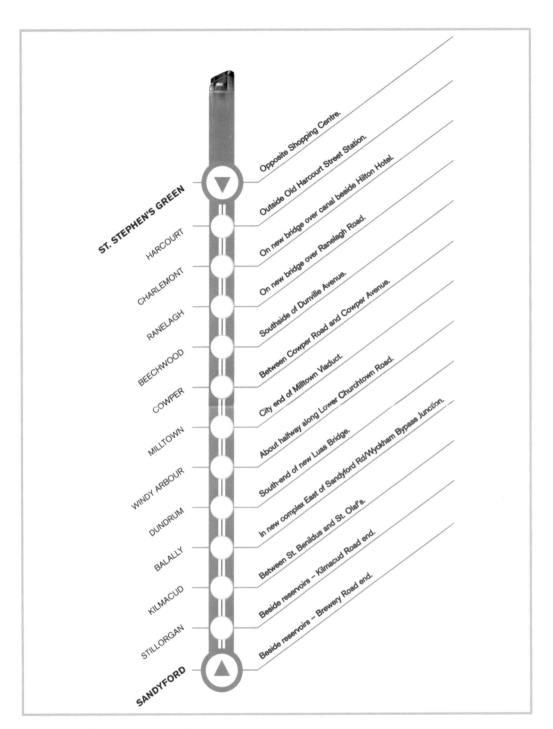

Map of the Luas Green Line

Preface

T he arrival of Luas on Dublin's streets this year has had a very positive effect on the city. Luas is already perceived as a superbly modern and efficient mode of public transport that is generating a new sense of pride in Dublin. It has won a remarkable degree of respect from other road users, who have come to accept the priority needed by Luas over other traffic because of the large numbers of passengers carried by the trams. While Luas was being built, other road users were understandably concerned about the potential for Luas trams being disruptive to traffic flows or were sceptical about the system's ability to handle traffic volumes on the first two routes to Sandyford and to Tallaght. The real experience of travelling on Luas has dispelled many of the old myths about Luas and has replaced them with positive comments and proposals for future extensions to areas of the city not yet being served.

This second book by Brian Mac Aongusa records the achievement of building a new state-of-the-art urban transport system on the foundations of the former Harcourt Street Line, closed and abandoned some forty-six years ago. It is both timely and welcome. The author draws attention to calls for extending the Luas system in a carefully planned way so that it could become a catalyst for greater cohesion and development, leading to an overall improvement in the quality of life in Dublin. That vision contrasts with the very nostalgic memories of the old Harcourt Street Line with which the author enriches a substantial part of his book and makes us realise the enormity of the changes that have happened over the past half-century.

Luas has exceeded our most optimistic expectations. Although enormous numbers of people were carried free during the first five days of travel on both the Green and Red Lines, over a million passengers a month have been using the combined lines since the introduction of full commercial operation. This level of traffic was not expected until the end of the first full year at the earliest. Clearly the travelling public has warmed to its newest mode of public transport and the substantial level of support already being given by the citizens of Dublin can only augur well for the future of Luas.

FRANK ALLEN
Chief Executive,
Railway Procurement Agency

CHAPTER 1

Luas a Reality

In spite of widespread public doubt, disbelief and even cynicism, Luas has become a reality in Dublin. After more than ten years in planning and construction, Luas trams have emerged as an elegant form of public transport of which Dubliners are now very proud. They grace the streets and routes to the south of the city and already the government is being urged to extend Luas to new routes around the city centre and to its northside. No longer seen as purely a fast and efficient mode of public transport, Luas is increasingly being viewed as a catalyst for cohesion and development that will lead to an overall improvement in the quality of life for the citizens of Dublin.

Luas was a long time coming, but it was worth waiting for. People living or working in the heavily-populated south-eastern suburbs between Sandyford and Dundrum are now within reach of St Stephen's Green in the city centre in less than 20 minutes. Those further south in the extensive suburbs between Tallaght and Drimnagh can reach the city centre within 40 minutes. These timings represent a substantial improvement on the same journeys that were taking twice as long until the introduction of the new fast Luas services in 2004.

THE LUAS TRAM SYSTEM

The excitement of Dubliners entering a Luas tram for the first time is truly palpable. 'Ah, Jaysus, isn't this grand altogether?' The features that most appeal to them are their surprising silence, their smooth running and their remarkable acceleration from standstill up to 70 km/h in the relatively short distances between stops. A further great attraction is the fact that they are powered by electricity and are free of fumes or smoke emissions. This environmentally friendly Luas has resulted from the meticulous care taken at the design and planning stages of the €775 million project that has produced what can only be described as a state-of-the-art light rail transit system.

A Luas tram arrives for crowds at Dundrum Station

A key factor in the success of Luas has been the decision to run on continuously welded rails, the new Citadis design of modern low-floor trams with resilient wheels and a high standard of suspension. These trams are capable of carrying passenger numbers greater than several standard buses and, thanks to rail guidance, can speedily penetrate the city streets right into the heart of Dublin. The high passenger-carrying capacity of the Luas trams justifies their dedicated paths in city streets and the priority given to them at road junctions. This ensures their high quality speed and reliable frequency.

The accessibility of the trams has earned much favourable comment. The 50m platforms at Luas stops are only about twice as high as a normal kerb and these allow a level boarding of trams for persons in wheelchairs and others whose mobility is impaired. Each end of the platforms is provided with a 5m ramp to facilitate access to level boarding. All Luas stops feature bilingual stop names, low platforms, shelters with seating, real time public information displays and bilingual ticket vending machines. Stops are monitored by closed circuit television and an emergency help point is provided at the side of each shelter to allow customers to contact Central Control in case of an incident.

The technology of the system allowing for rapid acceleration has facilitated the development of an efficient service with closely spaced stops located conveniently and within reasonable walking distance of many amenities. A glance at a map of the initial lines reveals how many highly populated suburbs have been linked together and with the city centre for the first time by the Luas service. The fact that the Rail Procurement Agency (RPA), which was responsible for building the Luas system, has projected that the Green Line to Sandyford and the Red Line to Tallaght should together generate twenty million passenger journeys a year emphasises the key role Luas is expected to play in the further development of public transport in Dublin.

FUTURE LUAS EXTENSIONS
The feasibility of extending the benefits of this new mode of public transport to areas and communities not already being served is actively being studied. The criterion in planning future extensions must be, of course, economic viability and that presupposes high-density population with regular transport needs along the chosen routes. A very

LUAS PRIORITY

The priority afforded Luas at road traffic junctions has given rise to some controversy. Naturally, motorists are irate at the clear priority being given to trams, conveniently ignoring the fact that the public transport vehicle can be carrying over 300 passengers compared with the private vehicle conveying at most 5 or 6 people. Users of Luas, of course, are very pleased with the manner in which their trams are being given priority over other road users at traffic lights.

The flow of traffic through light-controlled junctions is managed by Dublin City Council traffic controllers, who try to ensure that the flow is satisfactory to all providers of public transport. Under their system, a vehicle can be designated low, medium or high priority, depending on the time of day and its pre-agreed status in the traffic hierarchy. If the vehicle finds its priority setting is causing it to run late, it can request a higher priority which results in less waiting time at traffic lights. However, the Luas system ensures that the traffic controllers are given an automatic indication of a tram approaching a traffic light, triggered by the tram passing a certain point on the track. The second signal is sent as a request from the tram driver, who hits a button on his driving console. This normally results in a tram slowing down a little when approaching a red traffic light at a road junction, then as the light changes to green accelerating and gliding through unimpeded.

This unique Luas priority signalling system has attracted much interest and Dublin Bus are already discussing with the Dublin City Council the feasibility of introducing a bus priority signalling system similar to that used on the Luas trams.

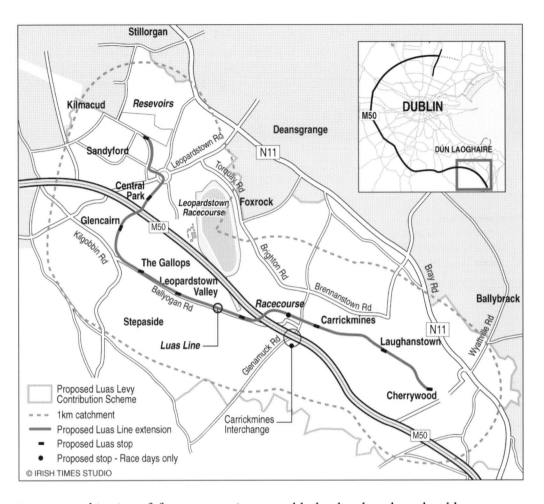

Proposed Luas extension from Sandyford to Cherrywood

important objective of future extensions would also be that they should encourage better and more economic use of land in future urban development. With these objectives in mind, the RPA has prepared extension projects for both Luas lines and these are already at detailed planning stage. It is expected that Light Railway Orders granting powers to construct the following new lines will be sought early in 2005:

- from the Sandyford outer terminus of the Green Line through Ballyogan to Cherrywood / Rathmichael;
- from the Connolly city terminus of the Red Line through the Docklands to the Point Depot.

Allowing time for the necessary public hearings of objections to the detailed plans and for the actual construction of the new lines, it would be reasonable to expect that these

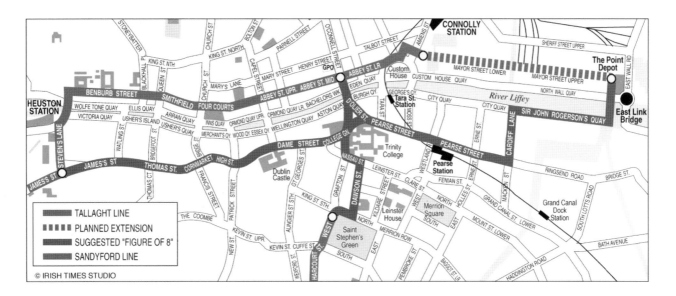

extensions could be completed by 2008. Their completion would significantly increase the potential of Luas in the Dublin region.

Suggested 'figure of eight' Luas line in city centre

The likelihood of further growth being stimulated by the Luas network has found expression in public suggestions for extending the system with the express purpose of achieving greater social cohesion and economic development in city centre areas. An example of an interesting proposal was that made by the acting Chief Planning Officer of Dublin City Council just one month before the official opening of Luas on 30 June 2004. In the course of a public lecture to the Urban Institute Ireland at University College Dublin, the City Planner Dick Gleeson, called on the government to connect the two existing Luas lines that had originally been planned as a single integrated system. He also suggested that an additional route linking the economic driver areas of the city – the International Financial Services Centre, Trinity College, Temple Bar and the Digital Hub – could provide a more coherent Luas network and would also help to redefine the urban structure of the inner city.

CENTRE-CITY LUAS CONNECTION

In a Cabinet reshuffle announced at the end of September 2004, a new Minister for Transport, Martin Cullen TD, was appointed. Just one month after his appointment the new minister, on 1 November 2004, in a *Morning Ireland* interview on RTÉ Radio 1, gave a clear indication of further positive development of the Luas network. Emphasising

LUAS LINES AND SERVICES

The present Luas system consists of two separate unconnected lines. Although originally planned as a single integrated system, the government decided in May 1998 not to approve the building of tramlines through certain city streets because of the disruption that would cause to centre-city business. Thus was created the unnecessary duplication involved in separate unconnected lines, with a consequent sharp escalation of costs now being conveniently forgotten.

The two Luas lines have been designated as the Green Line from St Stephen's Green to Sandyford Industrial Estate, following the trackbed of the former Harcourt Street Line for most of its way, and the Red Line from Connolly Station to Tallaght town centre following a completely new route via the Red Cow Roundabout, which has prompted this line's designation. The Green Line extends some 9kms south-eastwards from the city, has 2kms on street, 13 stops and 6 road crossings. The overall journey time from Sandyford to St Stephen's Green is 22 minutes. The Red Line extends some 16kms south-westwards towards Tallaght, has 5kms on street, 23 stops and 34 road crossings, with an overall journey time of 43 minutes.

Services on the Green Line operate over its full length at five-minute frequencies during peak-hours and at ten to fifteen-minute intervals at other times. A ten to fifteen-minute frequency is operated over the full length of the longer Red Line, but dedicated short workings may be operated between the Heuston and Connolly rail termini, to effectively increase the centre city frequency on this line. While there are no short workings as yet on the Green Line, operational facilities exist for such services in the crossovers provided between the tracks at Balally and Beechwood. On both lines services operate from 05.30 until 00.30 Mondays to Fridays, 06.30 to 00.30 on Saturdays and 07.00 to 23.30 on Sundays. Park-and-ride facilities have been provided at the Balally, Stillorgan and Sandyford stops on the Green Line and at Tallaght and Red Cow on the Red Line.

Despite the fact that the Red and Green Lines of Luas are not connected, both lines are treated as belonging to the one system by Connex, the company operating Luas for its first five years. Tickets bought for a journey starting on one line and finishing on the other are valid for the whole journey, without the need to buy a new ticket when boarding the second tram. Connex advises its Dublin users to allow 15 minutes to walk between Abbey Street on the Red Line and St Stephen's Green on the Green Line.

Platform carousel and Dargan Bridge, Dundrum

the importance of connectivity to improve the attractiveness of public transport in centre city areas, he said he was examining the early possibility of connecting the two Luas lines and also the options of further extensions to the Luas system. Questioned on a centre city connection between St Stephen's Green and O'Connell Street, the minister said he believed it could be completed within two years at a cost in the order of €70 million. This would seem to be a government endorsement of the success of Luas just four months after the Green Line began to operate services along the trackbed of the old Harcourt Street Line.

Urban planners see the great potential of an integrated Luas network that could be used to great effect in the future economic and social development of Dublin. They also see an expanded Luas system with much more on-street running in the city centre as a means of reclaiming the city streets primarily for the use of public transport. Private vehicles currently occupy by far the largest share of street space in Dublin city, leading to chronic traffic congestion that prevents the full potential of public transport being realised. An expanded Luas system would have the beneficial effect of restricting private motorists in city centre thoroughfares and encouraging them to make greater use of more rapid public transport. That would bring about a sea-change on the streets of Dublin and, with much less traffic congestion and air pollution, the general quality of city life would be greatly enhanced.

The prospect of a more environmentally friendly city is a very real possibility in the medium term if the government is prepared to recognise and accept the economic and social potential of an expanded centre-city Luas system. That prospect could not have arisen, however, had not the concept of Luas been envisaged in the early 1990s as part of a comprehensive and integrated transportation plan for Dublin. In turn, Luas would scarcely have been considered as part of that plan had not the trackbed of a former suburban railway to the south-eastern suburbs been available for re-use as a potential public transport corridor. That railway, fondly known as the Harcourt Street Line, was abruptly closed at the end of 1958 and abandoned shortly afterwards in economic and social conditions totally different from those at the beginning of the twenty-first century. The story of the transition from that old railway to the new Luas over the past forty-six years and of the Harcourt Street Line itself with its many memories, is recalled in later chapters.

Luas ticket

CHAPTER 2

Reopening the Old Railway

E arly in 2000, preliminary work was begun by CIÉ on clearing overgrown trees and vegetation from the abandoned trackbed of the former Harcourt Street Line. The actual construction of the new Luas line did not begin until March 2001 when, following a public competition, the contract to construct both the Sandyford and Tallaght Luas lines was awarded to a joint venture of the Italian company Ansaldo Spa, the Dutch group Ballast-Nedam and MVM of Australia. The Sandyford line contract included the depot at Sandyford terminus, the major cable-stayed bridge at Taney Cross Dundrum and track-laying along its full length, including street-level track from the Grand Canal to St Stephen's Green West in Dublin.

Far fewer difficulties than expected were encountered in the construction, as most of the work was along the old railway alignment. Some difficulties arose where the Luas line descended to street-level once it crossed the Grand Canal at the present *Charlemont* stop, which is centered on the new bridge over the canal. A curving ramp was built from the canal bridge to Peter's Place, allowing the new line to curve again into Harcourt Road, past the old Harcourt Street Station and down Harcourt Street to the terminus at St Stephen's Green / *Faiche Stiabhna*. Utility diversion works were necessary on the public streets before the Luas tracks could be laid and the below-street basement extensions of many houses on Harcourt Street had to be strengthened.

At the end of 2001, the Railway Procurement Agency (RPA) was established under the Transport (Railway Infrastructure) Act 2001 and it subsumed the role of the former CIÉ Light Rail Project Office. Early in 2002, the RPA began work on a new bridge over the Grand Canal at Grand Parade and, between November 2002 and April 2003, bridges were reinstated over Dartmouth, Northbrook, Ranelagh and Charleston roads at the

Refurbishing the old Harcourt Street Line trackbed for Luas near Dundrum

exact same locations as the old Harcourt Street Line bridges that were demolished in 1959. Rather than replace the former low overbridge at the old Ranelagh station, it was decided that the Luas line should ramp down to an at-grade crossing at Dunville Avenue where the present Beechwood / *Coill na Feá* stop is located. The new stop of Ranelagh / *Raghnallach* is located on the bridge over Ranelagh Road. The new *Cowper* stop is south of Dunville Avenue and before the old station of Milltown, at the site of which is the present stop of Milltown / *Baile an Mhuilinn*. Further south and beyond the restored Nine Arches viaduct of the old Harcourt Street Line is the new stop of Windy Arbour / *Na Glasáin* and about one kilometer beyond it the Luas Green Line / *Líne Uaine* traverses the magnificent new William J. Dargan Bridge before reaching the stop of Dundrum / *Dún Droma*, located exactly on the site of the old Harcourt Street Line station of the same name.

Just beyond Dundrum, in the former Harcourt Street Line rock cutting through an outlying spur of the Dublin Mountains, much rock removal work had to be carried out during 2002 and 2003. This was necessary not only to stabilize the sides of the old railway cutting but also to provide for its possible future use as a wider cutting for the planned Dublin Metro. A new bridge was built across the old railway alignment at St

LUAS TRAMS

The Citadis trams chosen for Luas were manufactured in La Rochelle, France, by Alstrom S.A. The standard tram of 30m used mostly on the Red Line to Tallaght can carry up to 256 people, 56 of whom may be seated. For use on the Green Line to Sandyford, this basic tram has been extended by adding modules of 10m built by Alstrom in Barcelona, Spain, to provide increased capacity for up to 358 people with 80 seated. All trams are of a silver / lilac colour with narrow yellow and broad purple bands at cantrail level.

The extension section consists of two modules: a centre car and a suspended car, the latter having two sets of double doors, one on either side. The centre car is carried on a low-floor motor bogie, while the suspended car is supported by the centre cars on either side and does not have a bogie under it. Therefore, the make-up of a Luas tram on the former Harcourt Street Line is: driving car with motor bogie, centre car with trailer bogie, suspended car, centre car with motor bogie, driving car with motor bogie. Inside, the trams are roomy and comfortable, with 360 degree views available through their large glass windows. Diagramatic route maps both in English and in Irish are provided over each doorway and 'bum rests' are available for standing passengers.

Of the initial fleet of 40 Luas trams, 26 are 30m long and the remaining 14 are 40m long. The fourteen longer trams (nos. 4001-4014) have been allocated to the Green Line and the shorter trams (nos. 3001-3026) to the Red Line. In height, the Luas trams are 3.27m excluding the pantograph, which is the arm reaching above the tram to connect with the overhead power lines. The trams are powered by electricity drawn at 750v DC and are capable of a maximum speed of 70km/h. Contrary to some newspaper reports, all trams are capable of being used on either the Green Line or the Red Line, as both lines have been built to the standard European gauge of 1435mm. However, there is a wider clearance between the two tracks on the Green Line to provide for possible future workings by Dublin Metro.

All Luas driving cars are fitted with attractive electronic gongs and a harsh horn as warning signals. They are also fitted with electronic destination displays constantly switching between the English and Irish languages. Green Line trams normally display St Stephen's Green / *Faiche Stiabhna* or Sandyford / *Áth an Ghainimh*, while Red Line trams normally display Connolly / *Conghaile* or Tallaght / *Tamhlacht*. When appropriate, Not in Service / *As Seirbhís* is displayed.

A Luas tram on Harcourt Street

A trial tram moves down Harcourt Street

Benildus College Kilmacud and, between March 2001 and August 2002, the Luas depot was built almost directly opposite the former Harcourt Street Line station of Stillorgan. The new Luas stop Stillorgan / *Stigh Lorgan* was built some 500m to the north and the first tracks were laid between this stop and Kilmacud / *Cill Mochuda* in September 2002, giving this section the distinction of being the first part of the old Harcourt Street Line to be restored as a working railway some forty-six years after its closure in 1958.

FIRST TRIALS BEGIN

The first of fourteen trams for the Green Line was delivered to the Sandyford depot on 18 February 2003 and was officially launched by the Minister for Transport Séamus Brennan TD on 9 March. All of the trams were delivered by the end of August. Following completion of the depot at Sandyford, extensive test running of trams took place from April 2003 between the terminal stop of Sandyford / *Áth an Ghainimh* and a

First Luas tram on test near Sandyford

point some 3km north in the cutting just short of the present stop of Balally / *Baile Amhlaoibh*. When the overhead power lines and underground cables had been further extended towards Dublin, the Green Line was energised from the depot at Sandyford as far as Dunville Avenue on 10 February 2004. The following day the first trams crossed the cable-stayed bridge at Dundrum, following a brief ceremony at the new stop just south of the bridge, and then proceeded to cross the Dodder River Valley over the Nine Arches viaduct of the old Harcourt Street Line.

A month later on 11 March 2004 the full extent of the Green Line from Sandyford to St Stephen's Green was energised and trams ran as far as the foot of the ramp in Peter's Place. It had been intended that they would travel as far as the terminus but because of the terrorist train bombings in Madrid that morning, the trial was cancelled as a mark of respect. The inaugural trial over the full Green Line took place on 15 March 2004 with trams 4002 and 4006 travelling to the terminus on St Stephen's Green West, where they were greeted by An Taoiseach Bertie Ahern TD and the Minister for

Transport Séamus Brennan TD. The trams halted at the new Harcourt / *Sráid Fhearchair* stop as a mark of respect for the former railway, whose terminal building still stands today directly opposite the stop and is known as The Odeon Bar. The two inaugural trams finally proceeded slowly down Harcourt Street to the applause of hundreds of Dubliners who greeted the arrival of Luas into their city with obvious enthusiasm.

Intensive running trials began on the Green Line following completion of road resurfacing work in Harcourt Street on 18 April. From about 09.30 until 12.30 on weekdays, trams operated every five to seven minutes from Sandyford to the city terminus, providing experience for the drivers newly-recruited by Connex, the operating company. These trials also enabled the RPA, which was responsible for the construction of Luas, to identify and eliminate teething troubles encountered by the experimental service. As the designated opening date approached, more intensive running of Luas trams over the entire day was undertaken and during the weeks immediately prior to opening, a full mock schedule was operated from early morning until late at night. This preparatory work paid off handsomely and ensured the enormous success of Luas from its introduction as a public service on 30 June 2004.

LUAS NAME

The name Luas (pronounced 'looass') is particularly apt for Dublin's newest transport system, as it means speed in the Irish language. But seldom do new street features escape the sharp wit of Dubliners. New statues introduced to the city's streets in recent years have attracted clever and amusing names such as 'The Floosey in the Jacuzzi' for the reclining figure of Anna Livia in a fountain; 'The Hags with the Bags' for the seated sculptured figures of two shopping ladies on a street bench; or 'The Tart with the Cart' for the much-photographed statue of Molly Malone at the bottom of Grafton Street. It seems that the new Luas will not long escape the attention of Dublin wits. Already it has variously been called 'The Jerry Lee'; 'The Daniel Day'; 'The C.S.' or, as the real Dubliners say in their distinctive accent, 'The Train in the Lane'.

Close-up view of tram indicator at Dundrum

▲ Marshalling passengers at
St Stephen's Green

▶

Two sisters boarding a Luas tram
and proudly displaying their
season tickets from the old
Harcourt Street Line

16

ENTHUSIASTIC WELCOME

The first day of Luas in public service was described in glowing terms on the front page of *The Irish Times* of 1 July 2004:

> Twelve years after it was approved by the Cabinet in 1992 and at a cost of around €770 million, the Luas had finally arrived to a hugely enthusiastic welcome. People converged on vantage points and lined adjacent streets to see it go by. At least 30,000 people travelled on it during its first day of operation, the numbers boosted perhaps by it being free up to and including Sunday.
>
> The level of interest was such that the intended 3 pm launch of public services was brought forward by an hour after the Minister's tram was mobbed by enthusiastic sightseers in St Stephen's Green. The operators had to increase the number of trams from five to eleven by five o'clock as the evening rush got under way.
>
> A spokesman said passenger numbers had far exceeded expectations. At one point in the afternoon, the frequency exceeded the intended one tram every five minutes.

During the first five days of free travel, some 440,000 people travelled on the Green Line along the trackbed of the former Harcourt Street Line. On the first fare-paying day, 5 July, it was estimated that 20,000 passengers availed of the new Luas service and during its first three months of commercial operation about 1.8 million fare-paying passengers travelled, greatly exceeding all estimates. With the end of the summer holiday season and the return of students to schools and colleges in September, the numbers climbed steeply and the frequency of trams at peak periods was increased to every five minutes, with a ten to fifteen minute service at other times. Unlike the former Harcourt Street Line, the Luas Green Line is now attracting consistently high passenger numbers throughout the day.

The reaction of regular users of Luas since its inception has overwhelmingly been positive. An information technology consultant working in Harcourt Street and living near Balally said to a newspaper reporter:

> Luas has cut my commuting time in half, maybe more. Before it came, my journey could take between an hour and an hour and a half. From my house it's a five-minute walk to the bus stop, where I could wait up to ten minutes. On a wet morning the trip could take up to an hour and twenty minutes – one day it took the bus twenty minutes and five changes of lights to get across the yellow box under the Luas Bridge at Dundrum.

The cable-stayed bridge at
Taney Cross, Dundrum under
construction by day
and at night

THE WILLIAM J. DARGAN BRIDGE

The building of a magnificent new cable-stayed bridge, designed by Roughan & O'Donovan, built by Graham Construction of Dromore, Co Down and directed by the architects of the RPA, was begun in June 2001 in parallel with the major road improvement works involved in the Dundrum bypass. This asymmetric single pylon bridge has a deck depth of some 1.3m and an overall span of 165m. It has a main span of 108.5m, a back span of 21.5m and two approach spans of 18m and 14m. A 50m high A-frame, or inverted Y, forms the pylon for the structure, which is rock-socketed into the underlying granite by 50 piles measuring 900mm x 22m. It proudly displays *Luas* at the top and can be seen as a significant landmark over a wide area of south County Dublin.

The bridge was built at one of the busiest road junctions in Dublin. It involved concurrent construction of a major new crossroads and bypass with the Luas bridge. Its construction involved much overnight and weekend working to minimise disruption to the major road junction, which needed to be open to traffic at all times. Thirteen pre-stressed deck sections of 3.5 x 13m each weighing 44 tonnes were prefabricated in Newry, Co Down, and trucked to the site, where each section was then glued together.

The concrete used in constructing the bridge contained 40% blast furnace slag, which helped to whiten the finish. Fifty-two stays are used to support the bridge and each contains between 19 and 35 strands of cable. A 10,000 tonne counterweight is needed to support the bridge. The last section of the main span was put in place, to the spontaneous applause of hundreds of proud Dundrum residents, on 4 August 2002.

Because of the enormous local interest in the project, the RPA organised a public competition in 2004 inviting suggestions for a suitable name for the new landmark bridge.

This evinced a significant public response, with 533 suggestions submitted. The RPA set up a committee comprising Jim Quinlan Chief Architect RPA; Brian Mac Aongusa author of *The Harcourt Street Line: Back on Track* and of this book; Sonia Drew Project Co-ordinator RPA; and Julienne Brown Planning Department Dún Laoghaire-Rathdown County Council, to review the suggestions. The committee recommended that the new bridge should be named in honour of William J. Dargan, as reflecting not only the largest number of suggestions received, but also as a fitting tribute to a pioneer of public transport in Ireland. William J. Dargan (1799-1867) is known as the father of Irish railways and was responsible for building the Harcourt Street Line, which has now become the Luas Green Line. He lived nearby at Mount Anville and was a regular user of Dundrum Station.

The magnificent new €9 million Luas bridge at Dundrum was completed three weeks ahead of its 56-week contract at the end of October 2002. It was formally named The William J. Dargan Bridge by his great-grand-nephew Fr Daniel Dargan SJ, in the presence of the Minister for Transport Séamus Brennan TD, on 19 July 2004.

Fr Daniel Dargan SJ and Séamus Brennan TD, Minister for Transport, at the official naming of The William J. Dargan Bridge

The view from over the shoulder of a Luas driver

Since Luas started, it takes no more than fifteen minutes to walk to the stop at Balally and then no more than twenty minutes by Luas to Harcourt Street. I'm lucky it stops just near my office.

A coffee bar manager in the Sandyford Industrial Estate was reported as saying:

I'm happy about Luas. My café is just around the corner from the Sandyford depot and with trams running every few minutes, people now have time to stop and have time to buy a coffee.

I can see people who used to drive to work now switched to Luas and the shorter journeys give them time to pick up a coffee and croissant. I used to have some problems getting staff because of the difficulty for people who live in town getting here for an early start. Solving that was a big plus for me. It must be for them too.

An estate agent in Dundrum also expressed great satisfaction with Luas for business reasons:

Luas has stimulated demand and pushed up house prices around here. For example, a three-bedroom house sold for €381,000 in Dundrum last November, but I'd have no problem getting €450,000 for it today.

Anyone who bought before Christmas 2003 is looking at a sizeable increase. There's a huge demand from first-time buyers, in particular, for former local authority houses in estates like Mulvey Park and St Columbanus. Both of these are close to a Luas stop.

In the early days of the Luas service, some newspapers and local radio stations organised competitions between various modes of transport over the same route traversed by Luas to determine how fast the new service was in reality. Although the results differed slightly depending on the time of day the experiments were carried out, they nevertheless produced remarkably similar findings. The private car travelling from the Sandyford Luas terminus to St Stephen's Green on a dry summer morning took 50 minutes. A Dublin Bus travelling on a wet morning from Sandyford reached St Stephen's Green in 53 minutes. A cyclist on the same morning got there in 34 minutes,

OLD WAYS DIE HARD

When Luas trams were first introduced to regular service on the Green Line and began running at street-level along Harcourt Road, Harcourt Street and St. Stephen's Green, it came as quite a shock that other road users had to yield the right of way to Luas and keep out of the street space marked *Lána Tram*. During the period of experimental trials, temporary bollards linked by plastic tape were placed along Harcourt Street at the boundary of the tram lane to prevent incursions from other road users.

However, when regular services began on 30 June 2004, these bollards were removed as a thick white line painted along the boundary was deemed to give adequate warning of the reserved street space for trams. Little did the planners know the strange behaviour of Dublin delivery vans. During the first week of full Luas services, these vans were frequently double-parked during delivery runs with

their outer wheels fouling the tramlines. This caused much agitated ringing of tram gongs that usually had the desired effect. But on at least one occasion when the Luas tram was trying to clear the way ahead, an arm extended out of a delivery van's window with its driver waving on the tram to swing out and overtake it like every other road user!

Luas safety signage

LUAS IN ADVERSITY

On the sunny Saturday afternoon of 28 August 2004, busy with holiday-makers and summer shoppers, Luas suffered its first major public embarrassment. Right in the heart of Dublin beside the St Stephen's Green terminus of the Green Line, tram 4011 arriving from Sandyford became derailed at the crossover points nearest the bottom of Harcourt Street. The derailment effectively blocked all tram movements there and caused a complete closedown of Luas services between St Stephen's Green and Beechwood for a period of over three hours. Major inconvenience was caused to thousands of Luas customers, many of whom were stranded in the city because their cars had been parked at outer suburban stops. About an hour after the suspension of Luas services, it was announced that Luas return tickets could be used on appropriate services of Dublin Bus, but those services were totally inadequate to deal with the substantial numbers of additional passengers seeking alternative transport.

In such a situation of utter frustration, bitter complaints and angry exchanges would have been expected from those returning to the terminus to catch their Luas tram home. Most surprisingly, that did not happen. As people arrived and saw the disabled tram splayed across both tracks, the most frequent question was 'Ah, poor Luas, what's wrong? Has she broken down?' When reassured that it was only a derailment, many elected to stand and watch while Alstrom technical staff arrived with their specialised lifting tools. Close on two hundred people formed a semi-circle around the rear tram coach that had totally left the rails. Then, good-humouredly, they observed and commented as only Dubliners can: 'Hey mister, how long will yiz be gettin her back on the tracks?'

Two hours of solid entertainment was enjoyed by the continually changing crowd as they watched every detailed move to re-rail the tram's rear coach. A portable generator to power the hydraulic jacks was first placed in front of the derailed coach and, once the power cables had been connected to the jacks placed underneath the tram, a long cord was pulled repeatedly to try and start a portable generator. At each failed pull, the crowd groaned a pitiful 'Aaahh!' Then a voice came from the back: 'Jaysus, it's like an ould lawnmower. Maybe it's out of petrol?' At that remark, someone unscrewed the fuel tank cap, looked in and sent for a young man with a can of petrol, which was carefully poured by funnel into the fuel tank of the generator. Then it strongly kicked into action and the assembled crowd cheered!

Each painstaking step of fitting various wooden blocks, coloured according to thickness, under the sides of the tram was discussed at length by the observing Dubliners, with comments: 'With all their bleedin' technology, what do they use but Lego blocks!' Of course, they also used hydraulic jacks which, in turn, were cheered on with: 'Looka, it's goin up and up and up. Now they're pullin it across. Jaysus, it'll take them all day that way.' Then a more sensible voice said: 'Yeh know, yiz are all feckin stupid standin there looking at it – it's just like watchin wet paint dry!'

Despite the fact that it took close on two hours to restore the rear coach of the tram to its rightful rails, the moment of final achievement was greeted with a spontaneous round of applause from the happy onlookers. Then individuals ran into the circle and personally shook hands with and congratulated the surprised Alstrom manager and his staff, who had skillfully achieved their difficult task in the full light of the public gaze. 'One thing', said a pensive onlooker, 'I wouldn't like to have to do me own work surrounded by a hundred of them smart Dubliners!'

Charlemont stop lit at night

but was 'a saturated, sweating and frustrated mess' by the time he reached the Luas city terminus. Only a motor-cyclist was able to beat the Luas time of 22 minutes, taking just 20 minutes to traverse the journey terminus to terminus.

The Luas tram system is a new phenomenon for Dublin and it will take time to realise its full potential. Already there is much evidence of its popularity as a modern mode of public transport and pride is being widely expressed in Luas as a symbol of a vibrant European capital city. If the political will can now be galvanised to link up the existing lines and implement a coherent and integrated citywide public transportation system with Luas as its backbone, we can be confident that the arrival of sleek and elegant low-floor Luas trams on the streets of the capital will lead to a long term improvement in the overall quality of life for the citizens of Dublin.

CHAPTER 3

Slow Awakening

. . . .

For ten years following the closure of the old Harcourt Street Line in 1958, there was an acceptance of the decision to replace the old suburban railway with a more modern bus service. But, with traffic congestion growing in the Dublin area, the reliability of bus services soon deteriorated. In fact, Dublin bus passenger numbers began to fall in the late 1960s. CIÉ began to co-operate with Dublin Corporation in special experimental measures designed to improve vehicle movement in Dublin. These included 50 extra buses added at peak periods, 29 additional suburban rail services and an experimental bus lane. The 1969/70 CIÉ Annual Report admitted that there was a significant increase in commuter traffic using suburban rail services in Dublin. A census taken in December 1970 among suburban passengers showed a daily increase of 14% on the corresponding period in the previous year. Commuter rail services were now increasingly recognised as important. Questions were being asked in Dáil Éireann about their possible expansion. Then the highly reputed international management consultants McKinsey & Company claimed that Dublin rail commuter services generated social benefits that far exceeded their operating losses. The tide was turning in favour of suburban travel by rail.

The most significant development of all affecting the future of the Harcourt Street Line was the decision taken in 1972 by Dublin County Council and Dublin Corporation to provide as an objective in the County Dublin Development Plan that the former line be maintained free of future development and of planning permissions. This was done to allow for the reinstatement of the trackbed of the line as a possible public transport corridor at some future date. Prior to the drafting of the County Dublin Development Plan planning permission had been granted for small parcels of land at Dundrum, Carrickmines and Shankill stations, as well as at Quinn's Road Shankill, but apart from these the former trackbed was kept free of development all the way from Adelaide

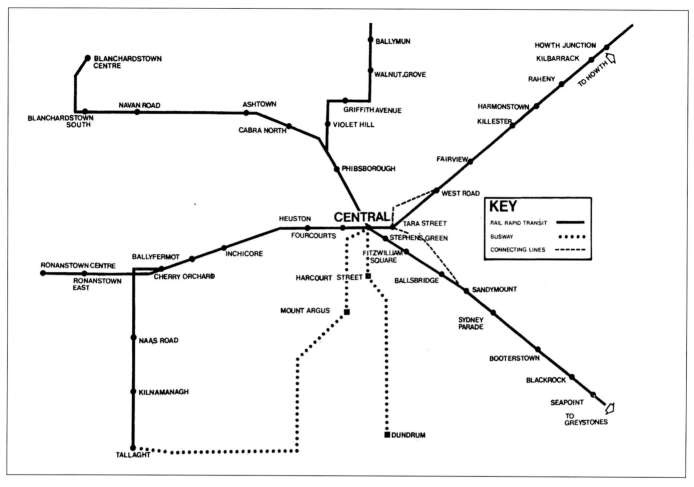

Road as far as the site of the former Shanganagh Junction. Had the Local Authorities not been so enlightened in 1972, the cost of reacquisition of the land needed to restore the public transport corridor to South Dublin would have been prohibitive.

By the early 1970s a consensus had emerged that suburban rail services needed development if Dublin's traffic problems were to be kept within tolerable bounds. In 1971 a preliminary study was carried out for CIÉ by the Dublin-based consultants De Leuw Chadwick and Ó hEocha on the electrification of Dublin commuter services and two years later CIÉ commissioned a new study to determine the feasibility of a Rapid Rail Transport System for Dublin, which could include some underground sections. Early in 1973 An Foras Forbartha published the Dublin Transportation Study recommending that services on the existing suburban rail links should be improved by

A DART train   increasing peak-hour capacity, providing car parking at stations and also feeder buses. By 1977 the Board of CIÉ had submitted detailed proposals to the Department of Transport & Power for electrifying the Dublin suburban Howth-Bray line, as a first step in a comprehensive Proposed Rapid Transit System for Dublin. These proposals, which were eventually approved by the government in May 1979, gave birth to the DART service five years later.

The relevance of the Dublin Rapid Transit System to the Harcourt Street Line was that it proposed using the former trackbed of the line as far as Dundrum for a dedicated busway. This embryonic proposal later gave birth to the idea of using the entire trackbed of the former railway as far as Shanganagh Junction for a Luas light rail system that could later be converted to a heavy rail Metro service.

Yet it took a long time for politicians to recognise the potential of the closed Harcourt Street Line. In a Dáil Éireann debate in April 1983 the then Opposition spokesman on transport, Séamus Brennan TD, argued for the construction of a busway on the old Harcourt Street Line from Shankill to Grand Parade on the Grand Canal. Nine years later, however, when he had been Minister for Transport for three years, Séamus Brennan – according to the *Journal of the Irish Railway Record Society* in June 1992 – said he could do no more than 'announce agreement in principle … to reopen a section of the former Harcourt Street Line as a public transport route subject to an ongoing feasibility study'.

The light of hope for reviving the Harcourt Street Line finally shone in 1994 when the retiring Chairman of CIÉ, Paul Conlon, spoke of a 'visionary government approach towards the development of public transport'. The CIÉ Annual Report for 1993 which he was launching stated:

> The National Development Plan sets the stage. The levels of funding negotiated at European level will enhance public transport services and ensure that public assets are supported and modernised… The recommendations of the Dublin Transport Initiative (DTI) to better the transportation environment in Dublin are additionally welcome and have the full support of the CIÉ Board. £200 million has been earmarked for investment in public transport development in the Dublin area.

Among the DTI's recommendations were further development of Quality Bus Corridors, extension of DART, new road development and traffic management measures, new park and ride facilities and the introduction of light rail transit routes, including one to Dundrum. At long last, in June 1994, it appeared that the Harcourt Street Line would be revived as a rail transport corridor.

The Dublin Transportation Initiative Report of April 1994 included in its wide-ranging recommendations that three light rail transit (LRT) systems should link the city centre with Tallaght, Ballymun and Cabinteely at an estimated cost of £300 million. In October of that year the government requested CIÉ to begin preliminary work on the establishment of the system and, as the retiring Chairman of the Board had predicted in June, allocated £200 million for this purpose.

After careful study of the available funding the following phasing was recommended:

Phase 1: Tallaght to Dundrum/Balally via the city centre;
Phase 2: Ballymun to city centre and Dundrum to Sandyford.

The Transport (Dublin Light Rail) Act was passed in 1996 and provided a legal framework within which CIÉ might apply to the Minister for Public Enterprise for Light Railway Orders (LRO) granting them powers to construct, operate and maintain light railways. The 1996 Act, however, required that a public inquiry be held in respect of each LRO application. In May 1997, just before the general election of that year, CIÉ submitted an application for an LRO for Phase 1 and the government committed additional funding for an extension of the Dundrum line to Balally and Sandyford. A public inquiry began in July 1997, but was adjourned in the light of political developments following the 1997 general election.

PROGRESS DELAYED

The new government elected in June 1997 decided to delay further progress on Phase 1, as it wanted to commission a report from consultants on the option of constructing the LRT system underground in the city centre. The report was commissioned in October 1997 and the highly regarded consultants W. S. Atkins reported in April 1998. They recommended that a surface system would be the most appropriate and cost-effective option in meeting the transport needs of Dublin and in providing capacity to meet long-term passenger demands. This report did not find favour with the government.

In May 1998 the government decided, contrary to the consultants' recommendations, that a section of the LRT system would run underground in the city centre between St Stephen's Green and Broadstone. On the northern side of this planned underground section would be a line to Ballymun and Dublin Airport using the former Broadstone railway alignment and on the southern side a line to Sandyford Industrial Estate along the alignment of the former Harcourt Street Line. The government also decided to proceed with a surface alignment from Tallaght but to extend it to Connolly Station. The new LRT system would be known in future as Luas, a word meaning speed in the Irish Language.

The government's decision effectively divided the LRT system into three sections which would remain physically separated from each other until the planned underground section was completed. The cost of constructing separate sections would be significantly greater than that of the originally proposed unified system, but this fact

28

LUAS Network

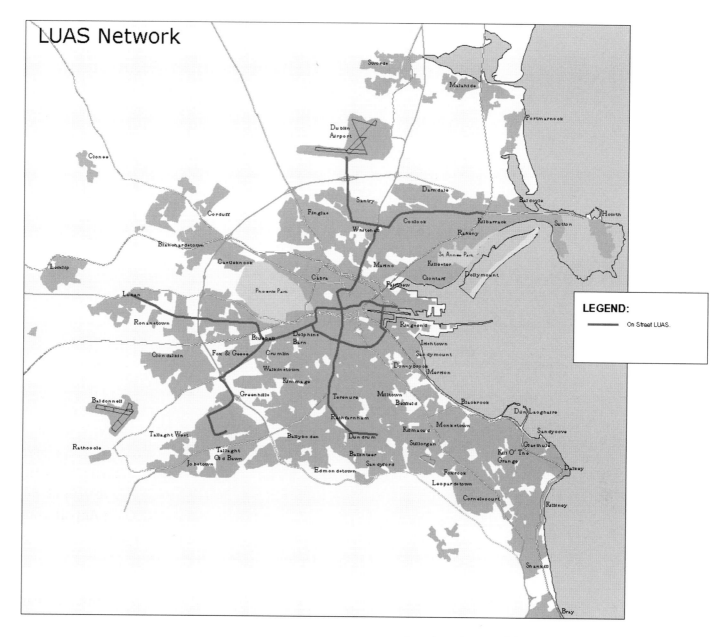

A projected map of the Luas network by
2016, taken from *A Platform for Change*
(Dublin Transportation Office)

was conveniently overlooked in the publicity surrounding the government's decision described as 'a longer term vision'. But that decision was cynically received by astute observers of transport developments and was severely criticised in an editorial of *The Irish Times* on 6 May 1998 under the heading 'Disintegrating Traffic Plans':

> After months – if not years – of dithering, no practical or realistic set of proposals is yet in place to address Dublin's chronic transport problem. Last night's cabinet decision to endorse a part-overground, part-underground LUAS – and to forego £114 million in EU aid in the process – is a dreadful example of political cowardice. It looks suspiciously like an attempt by government to postpone the evil day when the streets are dug up with the politicians taking the flak. The likelihood now is that not a shovel will be lifted – let alone a tunnel bored – until well into the next millennium. In an attempt to confuse the issue and provide themselves with political cover, ministers have turned the clock back to the early 1990s and reissued a version of the Dublin Transport Initiative's light rail scheme which includes a link to Ballymun, with an underground section in Dublin Central. This revived scheme has no designated start-up or finishing dates, although the Minister for Public Enterprise Ms Mary O'Rourke accepts that work is unlikely to commence before 2000.

In a letter to the editor of the same newspaper, the President of the Royal Institute of Architects of Ireland made the point that planning for the suburban rail systems was then one year behind schedule; two years behind for Quality Bus Corridors; two to three years behind for Luas; and four years behind for the Port Tunnel and completion of the C-Ring Motorway. It was a catalogue of failure by any measurement.

In line with the government's decision, CIÉ withdrew the applications it had submitted for an LRO for Phase 1 of the project approved in 1994 and prepared three new separate applications as follows:

Line A: Tallaght to Abbey Street;
Line B: St Stephen's Green to Sandyford Industrial Estate;
Line C: Abbey Street to Connolly Station.

A public inquiry, headed by His Honour Judge Seán O'Leary, was set up in January 1999 under the Transport (Dublin Light Rail) Act 1996 to consider the proposal for Line B and it reported to the Minister for Public Enterprise in June 1999. This allowed the minister to make an LRO for Line B along the former Harcourt Street alignment in

September 1999.

Due to the change in government policy towards the Luas system following the 1997 general election, a full two years was lost in the momentum generated for restoring a public transport corridor along the former Harcourt Street Line. Only in the autumn of 1999 could the CIÉ Light Rail Project Office set about implementing the plan for Phase 1 of Luas in line with the government's decision of May 1998.

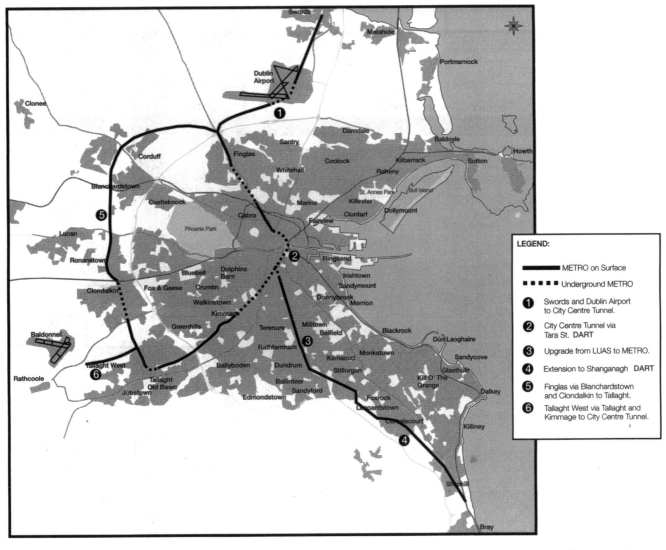

Map of proposed Metro network from DTO strategy

31

METRO PROPOSAL

Almost a year later, in July 2000, the Minister for Public Enterprise announced that the government had approved in principle the development of a metro system for Dublin on a Public Private Partnership (PPP) basis. The minister confirmed that Luas Line B from St Stephen's Green to Sandyford Industrial Estate would be constructed in accordance with the LRO made in 1999 but added that, in time, it would be integrated with the metro system. In September 2000 the Dublin Transportation Office (DTO) published *A Platform for Change: Outline of an integrated strategy for the Greater Dublin Area 2000-2016* incorporating the Luas and Metro lines previously announced. The government confirmed that it accepted the broad thrust of the DTO strategy that provided an overall planning framework for the development of Dublin's transport system in the medium to longer term.

The published DTO *A Platform for Change* has significant implications for the former Harcourt Street Line. The relevant paragraph of the strategy reads as follows:

> The METRO system will have a spine from Swords to Shanganagh. The line will run via Dublin Airport, Finglas, Broadstone, City Centre, Ranelagh, Sandyford and Cherrywood. The section between Broadstone and Ranelagh will be in tunnel and will interchange with DART at Tara Street. Construction of this line will entail the upgrading of LUAS Line B to METRO between Sandyford and Ranelagh.

Clearly it is now recognised that the alignment of the former Harcourt Street Line presents an ideal public transport corridor to serve the south county Dublin area in the medium and longer term. This recognition implicitly vindicates those who opposed the abandonment, as distinct from the continued operation, of the old railway in 1958 and emphatically confirms the far-seeing wisdom of Dublin County Council and Dublin Corporation who inserted as an objective in their County Dublin Development Plan as far back as 1972 the maintaining of the entire Harcourt Street Line trackway as a possible future public transport corridor.

An interesting feature of the DTO strategy is its provision for integration between the different modes of transport. It proposes numerous interchange stations on the Metro, DART and outer suburban rail, Luas and bus networks, including a fascinating interchange between the planned Metro and DART at Shanganagh – presumably the site of the former Shanganagh Junction which remains undeveloped. Some

Modern Luas tram passing new Sandyford depot

commentators have urged that the Metro should be joined to the DART line and continued to Bray, but these people do not realise that both the Luas and Metro systems have been planned to use the European standard railway gauge of 1435mm. (4 foot 8.5 inches), as opposed to DART and the remainder of the country's railway system which operates on the Irish standard gauge of 1600mm. (5 foot 3 inches). Interchangeable trains between Dublin's Luas or Metro and the rest of the country have not been planned, probably to facilitate the Dublin system being developed on a PPP basis and operated by private rather than public enterprise.

CHAPTER 4

Harcourt Street Line Closure

· · · · · · · · · · · · ·

The opportunity to close the Harcourt Street Line was created by the passing of the Transport Act 1958. In the summer of that year, it gave the new Board of CIÉ headed by the enthusiastic and energetic Dr Todd Andrews, the statutory means to deal with an unwanted suburban railway. Within six weeks of the board's appointment the decision had been reached to close the Harcourt Street Line on 31 December 1958. Only at the end of October were the travelling public informed of the planned withdrawal of services on and from 1 January 1959.

Over the following weeks, while rumblings of protest were being voiced, CIÉ steadfastly made their preparations for achieving an effective closure and rapid dismantling of the line. Mindful of the wanton damage caused by souvenir hunters and hooligans to the last Dublin trams on their final run to the Blackrock Depot some nine years earlier, CIÉ published the following small notice inconspicuously in the Dublin evening newspapers on 29 December:

CLOSING OF HARCOURT STREET LINE

On Wednesday 31st December 1958 travel arrangements will be as follows:

Train services will be withdrawn during the late afternoon and for the remainder of the day special substitute station to station bus services will be provided on which rail tickets will be valid.

CÓRAS IOMPAIR ÉIREANN

CLOSING OF HARCOURT ST. LINE

On Wednesday, 31st December, 1958, travel arrangements will be as follows:

TRAIN SERVICES will be withdrawn during the late afternoon and for the remainder of the day special substitute station to station bus services will be provided on which rail tickets will be valid.

CORAS IOMPAIR EIREANN

Last Journey from Foxrock

Charles Meredith lived in Foxrock and was a regular traveller on the Harcourt Street Line since childhood. He recalls that the railway was very important to the whole community in Foxrock. Almost everyone used the train in the days before extensive bus routes were developed during the 1950s. He was always very interested in the railway and enjoyed the leisurely lifestyle that prevailed in the days of the Harcourt Street Line. His own father who practised as a solicitor in Molesworth Street in Dublin regularly caught the 9.40am from Foxrock and returned from the city in the evenings on the 5.15pm from Harcourt Street. When one allows for a twenty-minute walk in each direction between the terminus and Molesworth Street, it becomes clear that the working day, at least for solicitors, was very much shorter in those days than it is today.

With great sadness, therefore, Charles Meredith observed the dismantling of the Harcourt Street Line during 1959 and 1960. He had the unique opportunity of travelling on one of the very last trains that left Foxrock. By the end of June 1960, the line had been completely removed from Harcourt Street as far as Foxrock and only the single down-line remained from there to Shanganagh Junction. On 28 June 1960, Charles Meredith travelled on the engine footplate for his last journey from Foxrock. The train, consisting of wagons of rails, sleepers and scrap, was hauled bunker first by former Great Southern & Western 0-6-0 Class J9 loco 354 with the late Matty Moore as driver.

Engine 354 on demolition train leaving Foxrock

They travelled to Bray, then along the coastal line to Amiens Street Station where their wagons of scrap were deposited, and finally to Broadstone Shed on Dublin's northside where the last train from the Harcourt Street Line ended its historic journey.

Those who spotted that notice in the evening papers began frantic enquiries to find out when the last train would run. As well as rowdy well-wishers and New Year's Eve revellers, there were many genuine patrons who wanted to make a final farewell journey on the last train. Most of these, however, were frustrated because the last train left Bray as early as 2.40pm in the afternoon and returned from Harcourt Street at 4.25pm.

The honour of taking the last return working on the line was given to Driver Ned Wheeler of Meath Road, Bray, one of five brothers who were all train drivers. Driver Wheeler, who had spent thirty-four years driving trains on the line, was joined by Guard Jack O'Sullivan of Wolfe Tone Square, Bray for the final run. Supervising the final day's events at Harcourt Street were Acting Station Master Frank Beggan and Foreman Michael Sherlock. The other trains on that final day carried only a fair number of passengers, but for the 4.25pm a six-coach diesel set hauling two extra carriages was provided. This well-filled train departed from each station to the echo of exploding detonators, but the crowds present were undemonstrative. The one notable exception

▼ Ned Wheeler of Bray, driver of the last service train

Signalman prepares to 'make the road' for the last train ▶

was the staff of the old Dublin Laundry at Milltown who turned out in force to see the last train and blew the laundry siren in salute as the it passed over 'The Nine Arches' for the last time.

On 1 January 1959 one of the former Harcourt Street diesel railcar sets was transferred to Co Tipperary to replace a steam train working the Thurles-Clonmel line. Other railcar sets from the line were used elsewhere on the CIÉ system in replacement of steam trains, thus making an immediate contribution to reducing losses on the national railway network. To coincide with the ending of the Harcourt Street train services, a new substitute bus route No. 86 was introduced by CIÉ between D'Olier Street in Dublin City Centre and Bray Station. Only 21 trips a day were provided by this route, compared with 23 trains a day. Moreover, the route taken by the bus was extremely circuitous travelling via Ranelagh, Milltown, Taney and Sydenham Roads Dundrum, Upper Kilmacud Road, South Avenue and Trees Road Mount Merrion, Stillorgan Road, Brewery Road, Leopardstown Road, Torquay and Brighton Roads Foxrock, Cornelscourt Road, Stillorgan Road (again), Moneloe Cross, Cabinteely, Loughlinstown, Shankill to Bray Station. No wonder the journey took approximately one hour – twice the time taken by a train which stopped at all stations. Following the Harcourt Street closure a much-improved train service to Dublin was provided for Bray and Greystones patrons travelling by the coastal line via Dún Laoghaire. Yet the fastest train from Bray to Westland Row on that line took 33 minutes, significantly slower than the 20 minutes taken by the former 8.50am from Bray to Harcourt Street.

ABANDONMENT ORDER

No time was lost in formally abandoning the closed railway and in disposing of the stations, tracks and bridges. On 8 January 1959, one week after closure, the CIÉ Board decided to set in motion the legal process. Within three months the Abandonment Order was made for Harcourt Street Station, which was then sold by public auction to the Hardwicke Group for £67,500 – at that time the largest sum ever paid for a property at an auction in Dublin. Immediately afterwards work started on the removal of the wide cast-iron bridge that spanned both Harcourt and Adelaide Roads and this was quickly followed by the removal of all other bridges as far as Dundrum.

This action effectively damped down any possible agitation for reversing the closure decision. By June 1960 the lifting of the tracks had reached Foxrock, but meanwhile two

▲ Closed Harcourt Street Station with 'Sold for £67,500' notice

▶ Inspector Jack Doran (centre) with staff at Dundrum during demolition

38

special trains were run over the closed line from Bray as far as Carrickmines in connection with the filming of *Johnny Nobody*, then being produced by Ardmore Studios in Bray. Dismantling of the Harcourt Street Line was finally completed in September 1960, with the salvaged track being sold for export to India. All of the property was disposed of by public auction and the sale of the station houses, adjoining land and scrap materials realised a total of £150,000.

In the aftermath of the closure the area surrounding Harcourt Street Station changed dramatically. In 1958 all the services needed by a daily flow of people to and from the station were provided by newsagents, fruit shops, hair stylists, boutiques and

Demolition by large crane of the Harcourt and Adelaide Roads bridge

Demolition of hair stylists near Harcourt Road in 1964

cafés, as well as those services available from opticians, chiropodists, dentists and doctors. From research carried out in 1980 by Rose Marie Daly, it emerged that the area around the former station had decayed significantly in the twenty years since closure. Many houses both on Harcourt Street and Harcourt Road had been demolished to make way for an inflow of office blocks that, in 1980, occupied 78% of Harcourt Street. Her research of *Thom's Directory* over the previous twenty years revealed some interesting facts. In 1958 over 20% of the houses in Harcourt Street were occupied by various medical professions, whereas that figure had dwindled to a mere 2% by 1980.

40

Schools of elocution, piano, dance, drama, etc. occupied 5% of houses in Harcourt Street in 1958, whereas only one such school remained in 1980. Similarly the buildings occupied by hotels in Harcourt Street declined from 14% to 2% in the twenty year period following closure of the railway. Harcourt Road had undergone a similar decline in economic fortune. 16% of houses there had been grills or cafés in 1958 and only 3% offices. The latter figure had grown to 40% by 1980 and the grills and cafés had virtually disappeared, leaving an overall impression of an area that had stagnated considerably since the demise of the Harcourt Street Line.

Those who today regard the closure in 1958 as being short-sighted do not realise that the population in the catchment area of the Harcourt Street Line has increased at least twenty fold in the intervening years. At the time of closure commuter traffic by rail was declining generally and a widespread belief prevailed that commuter traffic in future could more conveniently be handled by bus or by private car. During the 1960s, as the national economy slowly began to improve and ownership of a private car became possible for a growing number of Dubliners, suburban traffic on the coastal railway from Bray through to Howth was in decline. This situation continued until the end of that decade when increasing traffic congestion on the suburban roads began to move commuters back towards considering rail transport as the preferable option.

Early in 1969 the question of reopening the Harcourt Street-Bray line was raised in a Dublin evening newspaper. The desirability of having the matter discussed in Dáil Éireann was even publicly supported by the Chairman of Dublin County Council. CIÉ, however, were not enamoured with the idea and responded with the following statement on 17 January:

> This spur line off the main South-Eastern line suffered from the basic limitation of the remoteness of Harcourt Street station from the city centre, and it did not make a significant contribution to commuter transport. The three trains which arrived between 8.30 and 9.30am carried only 300 passengers between them and of these 100 came from Bray and beyond for whom alternative bus and rail services were available. Despite a 30% increase in rail travel during the last few years, the railways carry only 3% of all morning commuters. If the Harcourt Street line was still open and it now carried double the number of 1958, it would represent less than one half per cent out of the 140,000 travelling into the city every day.

View down Harcourt
Street in 1950s revealing
its remoteness

In an editorial the following day the *Irish Independent* described the CIÉ statement as a model of ineptitude. It said that by revealing evasiveness and a time-honoured display of passing the buck, the statement made all the more necessary some form of Parliamentary Committee. Correspondence followed for some weeks, but then the question gradually faded away.

CHAPTER 5

Why Did They Close It?

Dublin-bound diesel train at Foxrock with few passengers on platform

To a twenty-first century Dublin reader it seems inconceivable that less than fifty years ago a fine double-track suburban railway from Harcourt Street through Dundrum and Foxrock to Bray was hurriedly closed and quickly abandoned. Yet the demise of The Harcourt Street Line, as the railway was fondly known, was accompanied by little more than token rumblings of protest from a largely indifferent public. The CIÉ decision to close the line with effect from 1 January 1959, when announced at the end of October 1958, attracted relatively little newspaper coverage and was generally accepted at the time as inevitable.

Ireland's largest-selling newspaper, the *Irish Independent,* carried the proposed Harcourt Street closure under a single column headline. On the same page a four-column headline was given to the conferring of the freedom of the city of Dublin on the Bishop of Bathurst, New South Wales. An article entitled 'Prisoners of Chinese Reds' covered six columns, but the story that dominated page after page including one full-page photograph was the consecration of Cardinal Roncali as Pope John XXIII. The single-column Harcourt Street story read as follows:

Rail services on the Harcourt Street-Bray line will be withdrawn from January 1. Dr C.S. Andrews, Chairman of CIÉ, said in a statement the line had been operating at a loss for many years and its continuance had been decided on in pursuance of the directive that CIÉ must be self-supporting within five years… Dr Andrews said 74 people would be redundant as a result of the decision. The redundancies would be a matter for negotiation with the trade unions for transference or compensation for the workers concerned. The passenger traffic on the line totals about 1,000 a day. There is very little freight traffic. An additional bus service will be introduced between Bray and Dublin.

Todd Andrews

Todd Andrews

Dr C. S. (Todd) Andrews, the controversial full-time Chairman of CIÉ appointed by the government from 1 September 1958, was no stranger to the Harcourt Street Line. Before coming to work with CIÉ, he had been for many years a most successful Managing Director of Bord na Móna noted for developing the previously neglected peat deposits of Ireland to supply fuel for turf-burning power stations and for domestic consumption in the form of turf briquettes. Todd Andrews lived very close to Dundrum station and over the years that he worked at Bord na Móna headquarters in Pembroke Street, he was a very regular commuter on the Harcourt Street Line.

During the 1950s Todd Andrews must have witnessed the steady decline of commuter traffic on the line and the parallel development of improved bus services all along the railway route. He must also have noticed that use of the Harcourt Street Line by the affluent suburban classes was decreasing as they changed to private car transport, while continuing to send their children by the subsidised train service to attend fee-paying schools and universities. To 'a man of no property', as Todd Andrews regarded himself, the continued operation of such a service for the privileged few would have had little appeal. When it was demonstrated to him on his appointment as full-time Chairman of CIÉ that the Harcourt Street rail service could easily be replaced by the existing and expanding bus services, it was no wonder that he immediately supported management's proposal for the complete closure of the Harcourt Street Line.

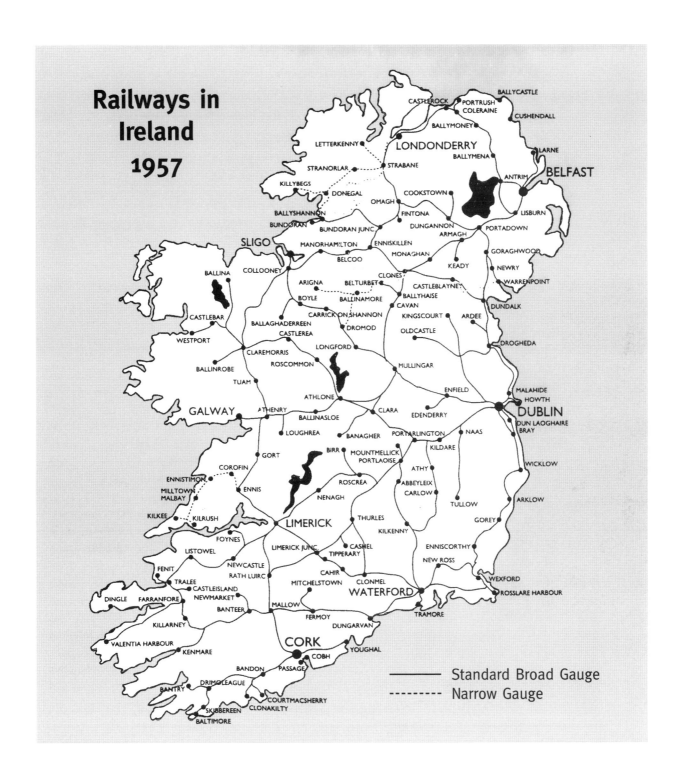

Railways in
Ireland
1957

Standard Broad Gauge
Narrow Gauge

45

THE BEDDY REPORT

The origin of the decision to close the Harcourt Street Line lies in the 1957 Report of the Committee of Inquiry into Internal Transport, chaired by Dr J. P. Beddy and known generally as the Beddy Report. That report considered the railways of Ireland in the 1950s on an extensive and authoritative scale. It found that the utilisation of CIÉ's railways 'was extremely low by international comparison' and sought out reasons that would account for that position. Its findings pointed to the decline in population since the railways had been built, a decline unparalleled elsewhere in Europe, and it noted the unfavourable geographic, demographic and economic factors pertaining to Ireland at that time.

To the modern reader accustomed to a recent long period of sustained economic growth, it is difficult to imagine the misery and despondency that prevailed in Ireland in the 1950s. Negative rates of economic growth were recorded during the middle years of that decade and Gross National Product (GNP) at constant prices was actually lower in 1958 than it was in 1954. Population fell in every year throughout the decade and employment nationally dropped by over 13%.

Against such a background it was not surprising that the Beddy Report found that the national railway structure was too large for the available volume of traffic. It pointed to visible evidence of under-utilisation on an over-elaborate railway structure in the many small stations handling very little traffic and adverted to the large numbers employed in relation to the traffic handled. When the report was published in May 1957 the summarised message carried in the media was that Dr Beddy recommended closing down over 150 stations and over 1,000 miles of line. Yet the report itself was careful not to indicate in specific terms the altered pattern of lines and stations that should result from the implementation of its recommendations.

Interestingly the leading articles of the national newspapers greeted the report's findings in a respectful tone. An editorial in *The Irish Times* under the title 'Facing the Facts' summarised the report and then revealed its own attitude to it:

> A nation as poor as ours cannot afford the luxury of a public transport system which is both outmoded and extravagant. CIÉ is being offered the only practical alternative – either to make the most important part of the railway network pay or to go out of business altogether.

The *Irish Independent's* leading article entitled 'Abandonment of Railways?' commented in a similar vein:

> The problem must be examined dispassionately. The horse has yielded on both road and farm to the motor vehicle. The waterways are almost abandoned as a means of transport. The tramway has been replaced by the motor omnibus. Has the time come when the railway must give way to motor services? The decision should not be influenced by sentiment, it must be dictated by the cold facts of finance and economics.

Apart from releasing the Beddy Report for publication, the Government did not make any comment. However in speaking to Dáil Éireann on 2 July 1957, the Minister for Industry & Commerce, Seán Lemass, gave the first indication that the government would have to consider requiring public transport services to be operated in future without subvention from the taxpayer. In the conditions then prevailing, that sounded the death-knell for the lightly-patronised Harcourt Street Line.

It must be remembered that 1957 was a bleak year, with Ireland in the depths of economic depression facing soaring unemployment and heavy emigration. The question uppermost in the government's mind was how the state itself, let alone the railways, could be made economically viable. CIÉ's financial results continued to disimprove with losses of £1.7 million in 1956/57 and its liabilities to the government reaching £16.5 million, excluding annual interest charges of £632,000. It was clear that a radical new approach would have to be taken to try and transform CIÉ into a relatively self-sufficient and financially viable organisation.

Post Office Mail

One type of goods legitimately carried by passenger trains until the mid-1950s was post office mail. Sacks of mail used to be delivered to Harcourt Street station each morning by a large wagon drawn by two fine horses and the sacks were lifted from the street to platform level by a lift in the yard to the left of the main station entrance. Mail for the villages along the Harcourt Street Line, as well as for Bray and Greystones, was put on the suburban trains. Jim Dowling remembers seeing a postman pushing a two-wheeled mail cart from the station at Dundrum up the Main Street to the post office, which was located where the AIB bank now stands. Outward mail was also pushed by hand cart down to the station each day. The practice of sending mail by train to Dundrum ceased in the mid-1950s when a new Central Sorting Office was opened in nearby Churchtown to serve the entire Dublin 14 area.

Poor shoppers in
Winetavern Street in 1953

1958 TRANSPORT ACT

A fresh start for public transport in Ireland was heralded in May 1958 by the new Transport Act under which CIÉ was relieved of its crippling interest-bearing debt and also of its nineteenth-century 'common carrier' obligations which in effect had required it to accept all traffic irrespective of its economic viability. While the 1958 Act did not stipulate any change in the railway network it imposed an obligation on CIÉ to maintain railway services and keep railway stations open, except where it would formally conclude that such services or stations had no economic future. Thus for the first time CIÉ was given statutory freedom to close uneconomic railway lines and stations without having to seek prior ministerial approval. Moreover to facilitate its reorganisation measures, CIÉ was granted an annual subsidy of £1.175 million under the new Act for a period of five years, but with an added statutory duty of ensuring that public transport would cease to require public subvention after 31 March 1964.

As soon as the Transport Act 1958 was passed by the Oireachtas the Minister for Industry & Commerce sought the resignation of the Chairman and other members of the Board of CIÉ. Then, with effect from 1 September 1958, he appointed Dr C. S. (Todd) Andrews – former Managing Director of Bord na Móna – as a new full-time Chairman of the Board who would also act as Chief Executive Officer. Dr Andrews effectively was now appointed to the supreme command of CIÉ with powers to achieve the stipulated goal of financial self-sufficiency by 31 March 1964.

Todd Andrews was well-known even before he joined CIÉ for his brusque and direct manner and was noted for his go-go energy. As soon as he arrived he quickly set out to reshape CIÉ with a firm resolve as may be gleaned from this extract from his autobiography *Man of No Property*:

> Experience soon confirmed my belief that the reorganisation of CIÉ was a crash operation which … required the virtually complete authority of one man. The Board was of course entitled to be kept informed of what the Chairman was doing … but the Board was not in a strong position to oppose whatever line of action he adopted. In the event of serious fundamental disagreement between the Board and the Chief Executive, I suppose either they or he would have to resign. In my term in CIÉ there were no such disagreements… I approached the task of managing CIÉ with great confidence and with a lot of goodwill from the public, the civil servants and the trade unions… My first act was to visit all the major railway and road transport centres and as many of the small installations as time permitted. I saw and spoke to as many of the staff as possible.

DECISION TO CLOSE
Within six weeks of his appointment as full-time Chairman and Chief Executive of CIÉ Todd Andrews presided at a Board meeting that received recommendations from the General Manager concerning uneconomic railway branch lines. The board agreed with

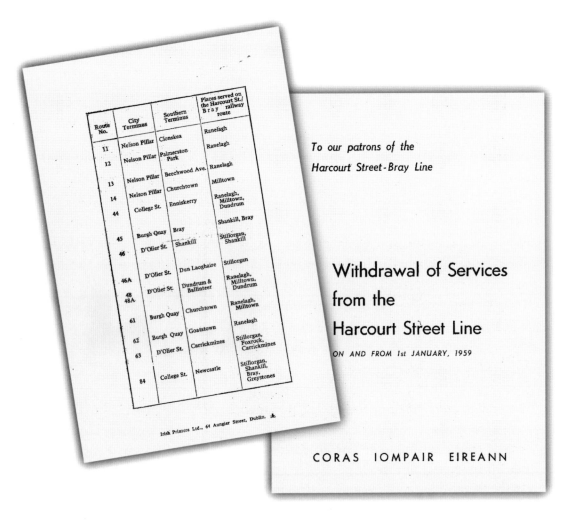

Cover of 'Withdrawal of Services' Statement

a recommendation that the line from Harcourt Street Dublin to Shanganagh Junction, just short of Bray, should be closed as the annual direct operating cost of the line was £77,000 compared with receipts of only £24,000 a year. The board also decided to issue a statement to all 'patrons of the Harcourt Street-Bray Line' explaining the need for withdrawing all services on and from 1 January 1959. This statement handed to all passengers at the end of October 1958 revealed that the estimated annual saving which would result from the withdrawal of services, and after providing for the cost of substitute bus services, would be £47,000. Furthermore, as a result of the withdrawal of diesel railcars and other equipment from the Harcourt Street-Bray section, the board would save a further £24,000 by using the railcars in place of steam trains in other

50

sections of the national rail system. Thus the full effect of the withdrawal of rail services from the Harcourt Street Line would be a reduction of £71,000 in CIÉ's annual deficit. The statement concluded:

> In view of these facts, it is hoped that the users of the service will understand that it would be impossible under the new conditions created by the recent Transport Act to continue to operate rail services on the Harcourt Street-Bray Line.

Refreshment at Harcourt Street Station

Brendan Behan   Myles na Gopaleen

The licensing laws in the days of the Harcourt Street Line allowed for the sale of alcoholic drink to a *bona fide* traveller even during the hours when licensed premises would be obliged to close for normal business. One of the stipulated closure periods became known as the 'holy hour' from 2pm to 3pm each day. In order to discourage excessive drinking, licensed premises were required to close at 2pm and send their customers home to have a mid-day meal. The licensed facilities in the Refreshment Room at Harcourt Street Station became so well known that they attracted numerous customers for the 'holy hour', all claiming to be *bona fide* travellers by virtue of having bought a train ticket for at least a twelve-mile journey. The playwright, Brendan Behan, wrote lovingly of this fine amenity in his newspaper column in *The Irish Press*, noting that the journey by train to Bray was just over twelve miles. Jim Dowling remembers a very unsteady gentleman trying unsuccessfully to buy a ticket to Bray around 2.30pm despite the fact that there was a long interval before the next train.

In November 1958, the renowned satirical columnist of *The Irish Times* Myles na Gopaleen was furious at the planned closure of Harcourt Street Station pointing out that 'under the station there is an immense cellarage filled with booze'. In fact, in the 1950s CIÉ operated a liquor museum in the vaults beneath the Refreshment Room. While the entrance from the street to this museum was at basement level, the exit was through the Refreshment Room!

REACTION TO CLOSURE

By and large, the general public at the end of 1958 was prepared to understand and accept the closure. The Harcourt Street Line had been steadily run down since the early 1950s as CIÉ developed and extended its city bus services into the south Dublin suburbs.

By the time the closure was announced no less than 13 bus routes were serving the areas surrounding the seven intermediate stations on the Harcourt Street Line. Many of the bus routes had a superior frequency to that of the trains and they terminated in the city centre, as opposed to Harcourt Street station over a mile away. It could well be argued that since the mid-1950s CIÉ had cynically desisted from trying any of the many suggestions put forward, such as a bus link from Harcourt Street to the city centre, to help improve patronage of the suburban railway.

In contrast to the attitude of the national media, the faithful patrons of the line protested strongly against the proposed closure and endeavoured to enlist the support of their local authorities and public representatives. Many supporters of the Harcourt Street Line criticised CIÉ for not attempting to experiment with more economic operational methods before reaching a decision to close the line. Extracts from letters to *The Irish Times* in November 1958 give some flavour of the public mood:

Tickets

A great variety of tickets was used on the Harcourt Street Line right up to its closure in 1958. Most tickets were made of stiff cardboard and printed by CIÉ with the names of stations usually shown both in Irish and in English. The accompanying illustration presents a selection of these tickets, which includes single, day return, excursion, platform, weekly and monthly tickets. Longer-term season tickets, which were handwritten on folded linen-backed cards, are not included.

An interesting feature of these tickets is that the Irish language shown on those issued in the early 1950s (nos.1, 7, 9 and 11) is printed in the old Gaelic script, while those issued in the final years of the line (nos.2, 6 and 8) bear the Roman script and standardised spelling introduced to schools in the mid-1950s. During the period of transition both scripts were used on tickets (nos.10 and 12). Another language-related feature to note is that tickets issued to and from Foxrock (no.9) did not show 'Cúirt an Choirnéil' as displayed on the station platforms. Instead the more colloquial name of 'Carraig an tSionnaigh' was used. It is also interesting that on tickets to Woodbrook (no.5), the golf club halt between Shanganagh Junction and Bray, no Irish version was printed presumably because of uncertainty in bestowing an Irish name on a private station originally opened in 1917 to serve cricket matches organised by the local philanthropic land owner, Sir Stanley Cochrane. Weekly, monthly and platform tickets did not carry bi-lingual names of stations.

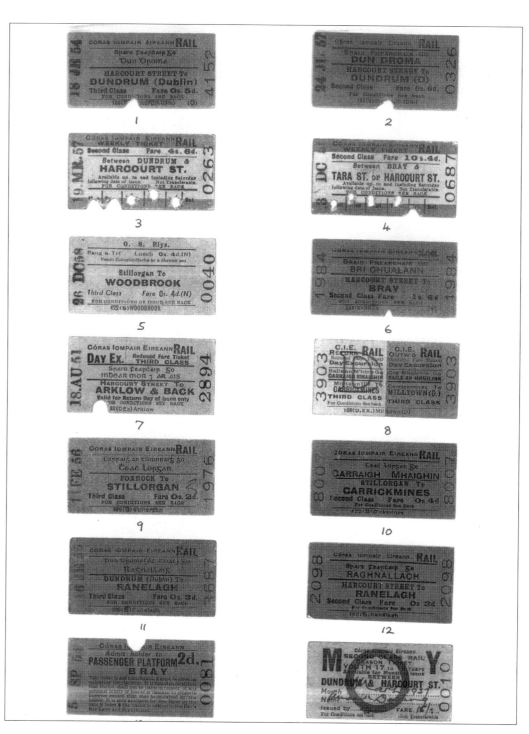

Examples of Harcourt Street Line tickets

The tracks to Shanganagh should, if at all possible, remain where they are. Whatever may be the wisdom of abandoning rural branches, it seems to be an act of criminal folly to abandon a suburban railway line leading from the capital of the State through a populous and ever-increasing residential territory like Co. Dublin.

★ ★ ★ ★

There is no doubt that the line has been allowed to run down and no serious steps seem to have been taken to try and increase receipts and reduce expenses. Receipts could be increased by providing better and faster services by lightweight railbuses, such as in Germany and as are being introduced in Great Britain. Expenditure could be tackled by running the line and services on an 'urban light railway' basis. Station staff could be dispensed with and tickets issued by a guard-conductor. Is it too much to ask that the experiment of an 'urban light railway' be made before the destruction takes place of an amenity which can never be restarted?

★ ★ ★ ★

It is common knowledge that weekly and season tickets on the line have been issued at a reduced cost so fractional as to be almost farcical, but even this has dismally failed to stem the decline in the number of travellers availing of the service.

★ ★ ★ ★

I have often seen trains on the line on which the passengers did not even mount into double figures. Yet I find there are 37 regular services each day; 9 others which run every day except Saturdays; and 5 Saturday-only trains.

Letter-writers to the *Dublin Evening Mail* often made much more blunt comments:

In the case of this line, one bus route after another has been set to compete against it until today it has to suffer the competition of 13 different bus routes. No attempt has been made to make any of the large new housing schemes available to the line, so that people living by the line could travel by train.

★ ★ ★ ★

As Mr Lemass said, it seems obvious the public are oblivious to the fate of the line. They are protesting now, but quite a number of them never travel by rail.

The proposed closure of the Harcourt Street Line was raised in Dáil Éireann on 7 November 1958 when questions were asked by various deputies who had been approached by patrons of the rail service. Speaking as Leader of the Labour Party, Mr Norton asked the Minister for Industry & Commerce, Mr Lemass, whether in view of the congestion on the Dublin-Bray road the minister should suggest to CIÉ that instead of closing the Harcourt Street-Bray line, it should try some imaginative propaganda to publicise the line and keep it open? There followed a fruitless debate which ended as follows:

A long diesel train from Harcourt Street approaching Stillorgan

Mr Norton: Something should be done to save the line which is one of the most popular in the country.

Mr Corish: The Minister does not travel on that line.

Mr Lemass: I see the empty trains often enough.

Mr Norton: I can see accidents on the Bray road to a greater extent in the future than before.

This Dáil debate was followed by a critical editorial in *The Irish Press* refusing to condemn the proposed closure of the Harcourt Street-Bray line:

> For so many years the railways have been such an enormous burden on the taxpayer that the Oireachtas have decided that, by 1964, CIÉ must pay its way. That decision must naturally involve reorganisation, the use of new equipment and the elimination of uneconomic rail services... Yet in the Dáil recently three Opposition Deputies could ignore the economics and practical facts of the case and press that the line, regardless of losses, be kept open. The public, by withdrawing their support from the Harcourt Street Line over the years, has given the real answer to protests of this kind. The travelling public prefer other kinds of transport and they have given their decision.

DEBATES BY LOCAL AUTHORITIES

In November 1958 Dublin County Council debated the proposed closure, but also refused to condemn it. The chairman suggested that the Council should not lose sight of the fact that the Harcourt Street Line represented a loss to CIÉ of £71,000 a year – proof that people did not want it. The chairman added that he did not favour a motion that would have the effect of maintaining such a heavy loss. The council agreed instead to ask CIÉ to defer closing the Harcourt Street-Bray line until alternative transport was provided.

An interesting insight to public attitude towards the Harcourt Street Line may be found in extensive reports in the *Wicklow People* of debates at meetings of Bray Urban District Council during November 1958. Clearly some councillors had been lobbied by patrons of the rail service to organise a public meeting to protest against the planned closure, but their efforts received only a lukewarm welcome. One councillor, who said he had travelled very much on the railway but had by then elected to travel by road, believed the people of Bray had turned their backs on the railway people and had let

The unusual two-armed signal at Tully Gates

the railway workers down. He said railways were outdated for suburban travel and even in Bray people living at the northern or southern end were not going to travel on an infrequent train service when they had a bus every ten minutes. Another councillor felt the fault lay to a certain extent with CIÉ. They failed to modernise rail travel. He saw large trains running infrequently during the day, when a number of smaller diesel trains run more frequently would better suit the public's need. The Harcourt Street Line had a huge potential for new customers in the housing schemes at Dundrum, Milltown and Stillorgan but CIÉ had let the buses steal them.

Some councillors said they could not work up sufficient enthusiasm for the suggested public protest meeting. Almost everyone in the council had sacrificed the trains for cars or buses and they themselves were responsible for CIÉ's proposed closure. If the people wanted the Harcourt Street Line they could have it, but they had forsaken it. Bray Urban District Council finally decided to seek more facts and figures concerning the proposed closure before agreeing to hold a public protest meeting. As the *Wicklow People* reported, doubts persisted that the protest might not be as strong as people may think.

It is clear that the Harcourt Street Line was quickly closed by the Board of CIÉ at the end of 1958 primarily to make a significant contribution towards reducing its overall railway losses and to comply with the stern conditions imposed by the 1958 Transport Act. The secondary reason was probably to set a strong precedent in the capital city for closing down an uneconomic railway, so that it would ease the political problems of further extensive closures then being planned for large areas outside Dublin. The reduction in railway lines actually achieved by 1964 by the Board of CIÉ amounted to 29% of its total network involving the closure of no less than 218 stations throughout the country. A third and significant reason for closing the Harcourt Street Line on 31 December 1958 was that the majority of the travelling public had gradually withdrawn their custom from a line that had been seriously rundown in the economically depressed years of the 1950s. Unfortunately the remaining small minority of loyal patrons did not succeed in generating sufficient public interest in preserving what undoubtedly was an invaluable public transport asset in South County Dublin.

CHAPTER 6

'Sea Breeze' Excursions

T o the ordinary Dubliner in the depressed 1950s, a chance to get to the seaside was as great a thrill as a chance today of going on a flight to Spain for a holiday in the sun. Most people then could not afford to go away during their annual two weeks' holidays from work. Only the very privileged could afford to rent a seaside cabin in Bray. The majority yearned for a chance to get to the seaside as cheaply as possible on a day excursion during the summer, hoping always that it would not rain and spoil their fun.

The railway companies in Ireland had a long tradition of offering both urban and rural people opportunities of cheap fares for outings on weekly half-day holidays, at weekends and on occasions of important local events, such as fairs or pilgrimages. The Harcourt Street Line was no exception in this regard and it had built up a reputation for regular enjoyable excursion trains run to suit the inner city dwellers of Dublin. In the 1920s cheap fares were offered for 'School and Pic-Nic Parties' from Harcourt Street to Foxrock, Carrickmines, Shankill and Bray, as well as to Greystones and Wicklow, while in the 1930s day excursion trains to Woodenbridge in the Vale of Avoca in Co Wicklow included a 'dancing car' in which passengers passed the time dancing and drinking. In the 1950s special day-excursion trains were run from Harcourt Street to motor racing on the Wicklow Circuit and to yachting at the Annual Wicklow Regatta.

During the 1950s it was customary for most shops in Dublin to close down for a half-day every Wednesday afternoon and for most offices to have a half-day on Saturday afternoons. This provided a potential market for rail excursion traffic and in July 1950, after an absence of eleven years, CIÉ restored the famous 'Sea Breeze' excursion train of pre-Second World War days from Harcourt Street to Wicklow and Arklow every Wednesday and Saturday during July and August. For only three shillings to Wicklow and five shillings to Arklow, one could buy a return ticket that would allow up to five hours by the sea – a wonderful opportunity in those days before extensive ownership

▲ Double-headed 'Sea Breeze'
passing Foxrock in 1953

▶

GSR notice of cheap fares for
'School and Pic-Nic Parties'

▶

Advertisement for 'Sea Breeze'
Excursion Trains

GREAT SOUTHERN RAILWAYS

CHEAP FARES

FOR

School and Pic-Nic Parties

FROM

DUBLIN TO DALKEY, KILLINEY, BRE
(BRAY), etc.   ::   ::   ::

DUBLIN To	SCHOOL			PIC-NIC PARTIES					
	25 to 50	51 to 100	Over 100	10 to 20		21 to 40		41 to 100	
	3RD CLASS			1st	3rd	1st	3rd	1st	3rd
FOXROCK ..	3d.	3d.	3d.	10d.	6d.	10d.	6d.	8d.	5d.
DALKEY	3d.	3d.	3d.	10d.	6d.	10d.	6d.	8d.	5d.
CARRICKMINES SHANKILL }	4d.	4d.	4d.	1/4	9d.	1/4	9d.	1/2	8d.
KILLINEY ..	4d.	4d.	4d.	1/2	9d.	1/2	8d.	1/-	8d.
BRÉ (Bray) ..	6d.	6d.	5d.	1/9	1/-	1/6	10d.	1/3	9d.
GREYSTONES ..	8d.	8d.	7d.	2/5	1/5	2/3	1/3	2/-	1/-
WICKLOW ..	2/-	1/9	1/6	7/-	4/-	6/-	3/6	5/6	3/-

To obtain above, application must be made by letter, not less than two
days before the Excursion, to the Commercial Manager, Kingsbridge, Dublin.

M. F. KEOGH,
General Manager.

DUBLIN, APRIL, 1927.

SEA BREEZE EXCURSION TRAINS

FROM HARCOURT STREET, 3 P.M.

TO ARKLOW   TO WICKLOW
5/- - -   3/-

EVERY Wednesday and Saturday, to August 27th. Timetable
and 3rd Class Excursion Fares.

Depart	p.m.	To Arklow s. d.	To Wicklow s. d.
HARCOURT STREET	3.06	5 0	3 0
Bray	3.31	4 0	2 0
Greystones	3.47	3 6	1 3
WICKLOW	4.03	2 6	—
Glenealy	4.19	1 9	—
Rathdrum	4.30	1 6	—
Avoca	4.44	1 0	—
Woodenbridge	4.50	9	—
ARKLOW	5.00	—	—

Return train from Arklow at 8.15 p.m., Wicklow 9.10 p.m.;
arrive Harcourt St., 10.14 p.m.
Cheap Day Excursion Tickets will also be issued for travel
to Wicklow and Arklow from Stations Amiens Street to Killiney,
inclusive, by the 2.30 p.m. train from Amiens St. On return
journey, passengers from these stations change at Bray and
travel on 10.05 p.m. and 10.20 p.m. trains from Bray to stations
served.

CORAS IOMPAIR EIREANN

of private cars had developed. Because of the very cheap fares offered, the 'Sea Breeze' excursions became immensely popular. In the fine summer of 1955 capacity crowds were regularly carried, with extra excursions being run on some Sundays in the height of the season.

In the 1950s the 'Sea Breeze' departed from Harcourt Street in an atmosphere highly charged with excitement and emotion. Long queues of mothers, fathers and their large families of boisterous children together with prams and go-cars would often extend from the ticket booking office in the Main Hall down Harcourt Street as far as Hatch Street corner. When the head of the queue was reached and the tickets purchased, there would follow a veritable stampede up the stairs, while the more agile and smarter children would rush along the single wide platform frantically searching for seats in the individual compartments of the very long train, usually made up of older six-wheel carriages hauled by two hissing vintage steam engines.

Harcourt Street Station and Beckett

Dr Eoin O'Brien in his major study *Beckett Country* maintains that Harcourt Street Station is of major importance in the works of Samuel Beckett. In an *Evening Telegraph* article, Beckett described the station as possessing

> A little piazza of sixteen Tuscan pillars, broken in the middle by a large round arch surmounted by a pediment. It has one platform only, so that incoming and outgoing trains have to play at 'Box and Cox' perpetually. On most occasions indeed, it is truer to say that trains come in merely to go out again.
>
> (*Coming from the Country*, 13 June 1924)

The desultory atmosphere of the waiting room at Harcourt Street terminus permitted Beckett to contemplate the meaning of waiting:

> And what if all this time I had not stirred hand or foot from the third class waiting room of the South-Eastern Railway Terminus, I never dared wait first on a third class

ticket, and were still there waiting to leave, for the south-east, the south rather, east lay the sea, all along the track, wondering where on earth to alight, or my mind absent, elsewhere. The last train went at twenty-three thirty, then they closed the station for the night. What thronging memories, that's to make me think I'm dead, I've said it a million times.

> (*Texts for Nothing*, p. 94)

Samuel Beckett visited Dublin after the closure of the station and sadness is reflected in his poignant prose:

> No getting out to it that way so what next no question of asking not another word to the living as long as you lived so foot it up in the end to the station bowed half double get out to it that way all closed down and boarded up Doric terminus of the Great Southern and Eastern all closed down and the colonnade crumbling away so what next.
>
> (*That Time*, p. 231)

Harcourt Street Station during the 1940s

Despite the shouts and screams of panic and excitement, all of this frenetic activity of people and prams was accepted with much good humour by almost all of the staff, from the Station Master and Station Foreman to the Ticket Checkers and Platform Inspectors. Only the Boy Porters were disgruntled as they had the unenviable task of closing and locking compartment doors repeatedly as more and more people changed their minds in the fuss and bother of finding empty seats in an already well-filled train. Finally, at the appointed hour, with a long blow of his whistle and a wave of his green flag, the guard would signal to the driver that he could sound the engine's shrill whistle and depart with high hopes for the seaside and sunny weather.

But the 'Sea Breeze' was not immune to the problems afflicting old steam engines in the 1950s. This letter from the *Evening Herald* of 27 July 1955 tells its own story:

62

Station Master Bowe (r)
with Foreman Murphy (l)
at Harcourt Street

Crews of 'Race Specials' in front of Loco 651 at Harcourt Street in January 1954. From left to right: Jack Silver, Paddy Murphy, Jack Wheeler and Larry Kearney

I took the 'Sea Breeze' excursion to Arklow last Sunday. Leaving Harcourt Street at 1.45pm we arrived in Wicklow 30 miles distant at 3.30pm. The next ten miles from Wicklow to Rathdrum took fifty minutes. Admittedly it is mostly uphill and we had long stops at Rathnew, Glenealy and Rathdrum. The majority of the passengers disembarked at these stations to form dancing parties, etc. For myself, I bought, wrote and posted a few dozen postcards.

Avoca 43 miles from Dublin signalled our approach at 4.30pm Still there were no complaints. The Irish countryside shone resplendent in glorious sunshine. With everyone in happy mood, it was accepted that Arklow would be reached eventually. I left the train at Avoca to commence a cycling itinerary.

I arrived back in Avoca with ample time to resume my meanderings on the 'Sea Breeze'. This time the train was drawn by two engines. Leaving Avoca at almost 10pm it took us nearly three hours to reach Harcourt Street on Monday morning at 12.30am.

In fact, the return 'Sea Breeze' that evening was drawn by two ageing engines – the former Midland & Great Western 2-4-0 locomotive 652 built in 1898 and the former Dublin & South Eastern 0-6-0 locomotive 445 built in 1908.

64

CHAPTER 7

Trains and Travellers

· ·

Uniquely in Ireland the Harcourt Street line had three different types of motive power – steam trains, electric battery trains and diesel power. Up to 1932 steam engines hauled all trains but in that year the Great Southern Railways (GSR) – precursor to Córas Iompair Éireann (CIÉ) – introduced a two-coach articulated train set powered by electric storage batteries to the Harcourt Street-Bray service. A second train set was soon added and in 1939 two further and more modern sets were introduced. These electric battery trains operated on the line for seventeen years until 1949 and became popularly known as 'The Drumm Trains'. In the 1950s when CIÉ began to replace its ageing steam engines with diesel motive power, consideration was given to finding a more economic method of working the loss-making Harcourt Street Line. Late in 1954 some of the newly-arrived mainline diesel railcars were tried on the line and, as these proved satisfactory, a number of the railcars were adapted for suburban working by removing the toilet compartments and substituting extra seating. By the end of 1955, three adapted sets were sent to operate on the Harcourt Street-Bray service in the hope of achieving the desired economic objective.

Steam and Diesel Workings

Compared with the coastal line from Bray to Amiens Street, the Harcourt Street Line was more steeply graded and required stronger steam locomotives to haul heavily-loaded trains. The provision of motive power in the 1950s was the responsibility of Bray Engine Shed. It took five engines to operate the service on the line and these tended to be larger locomotives with coal tenders rather than smaller tank engines. The most common steam motive power on the Harcourt Street Line was the former Great Southern & Western J15 0-6-0 locos of the 101 class such as 166, 186 or 188, closely followed by the former Midland & Great Western G2 2-4-0 locos such as 651, 657, 661 or 665.

As these locos were mostly built in the nineteenth century, efforts were made to replace them in the case of heavier trains with the more modern Great Southern Railways J15B 0-6-0 locos of the 710 class built in the 1930s such as 712, 713 or 717. For express trains, such as the 8.50am

65

Double-headed steam train crossing 'The Nine Arches'

from Bray or the 6.05pm Arklow train that ran non-stop from Harcourt Street to Bray, engines with larger driving wheels were used, such as former Great Southern & Western D14 4-4-0 locos 61 (in green livery), 63 or 89 and D4 4-4-0 locos 335, 342 or 346. The former Dublin & South Eastern J8 0-6-0 locos such as 444 and 445, as well as K2 2-6-0 locos 461 and 462 normally used on the Wexford goods trains, were also occasionally rostered to work trains on the Harcourt Street Line.

Tank engines of various classes were used on the lighter suburban trains, including former Dublin & South Eastern F1 2-4-2T locos 435 and 436, C2 4-4-2T loco 455 (in green livery) and former Cork Bandon & South Coast B4 4-6-0T loco 466. Occasionally the more modern Great Southern Railways I3 0-6-2T locos 670 and 674 or P1 2-6-2T

outside cylinder 850 (in green livery) were used mainly for 'Race Specials' from Harcourt Street to Foxrock for Leopardstown race meetings.

With regard to diesel workings, modern AEC diesel railcars started taking over suburban services on the Harcourt Street Line from late in 1954. In summer 1956, Metro-Vickers 1,200hp A class diesel-electric locomotives began to take charge of 'Sea Breeze' excursions and the summer mainline trains to Rosslare. The smaller Metro-Vickers 550hp C class diesel-electric locomotives were tried for suburban services, but did not prove reliable or suitable for the heavily graded line. Following conversion of Bray Shed to diesel operation in June 1957, a number of A and C class locos were assigned to regular workings on the line. In May and June 1958, Maybach diesel loco E418 made a

66

Loco 86 with large driving wheels on Arklow train at Bray

Diesel loco A32 on Rosslare train at Harcourt Street with train catering staff Paddy Miller and Charlie Rowe of Rosslare with Foreman 'Corky' Murphy

number of trial runs on the line with five bogie coaches, but this class of diesel loco was not used on regular services.

After an initial period on the Harcourt Street Line, the mainline railcars were replaced by suburban railcars that could each accommodate 12 first class and 36 third class passengers. Many of these suburban railcars within the numbers 2648-2657 were used on the line fitted with special bus-type seating. The final train to run on the Harcourt Street Line on 31 December 1958 consisted of railcar 2653, coach 2169, railcar 2648, railcar 2655, coach 2163 and railcar 2650, hauling two extra coaches 808 and 1306.

Patrons of the Harcourt Street Line had the questionable privilege during the 1950s of travelling either in antique rough-riding wooden carriages, which many believed had 'square wheels', hauled by equally ancient hissing steam engines or of joining a sleek modern diesel railcar – depending on which train happened to come along at a particular time of the day. To give some flavour of the annoyance caused to regular passengers by the ancient carriages, the following extract from a letter to the Dublin *Evening Mail* on 21 August 1954 is illuminating:

On any wet day go to any suburban station and you will see the unfortunate travellers searching for a coach in which the roof is not leaking. It is a pity that CIÉ do not throw a tarpaulin over the top of each carriage on wet days. Certainly the 'speed' of the trains would not blow the tarpaulin off the roof.

Another bitter complaint made to the *Evening Mail* belied the publicity of CIÉ's slogan at that time – 'Travel by Train for Speed and Comfort':

Tuesday 17/8/1954 as Dubliners are aware was a day of heavy rain and storm from early morning. The return lunch-time train was 12 minutes late and unfortunates having trudged to the station in the rain had to trudge back and seek some other mode of conveyance.

A further complaint highlights the patrons' lingering suspicion of CIÉ's real intentions:

Would CIÉ please say why they are trying to drive people from travelling regularly on their line. If they want to close down this particular line of suburban trains why have they not the moral courage to say so instead of inflicting every sort of discomfort on the unfortunate weekly and season ticket holders.

The typical carriages of the steam-hauled trains in the first half of the 1950s were well described in his recollections of the line by the late J.P. O'Dea in the *Irish Railway Record Society Journal* in October 1988:

On the track next to the wall in Harcourt Street station stood a rake of Dublin & South Eastern (pre-1925) gas-lit six-wheelers. Some of the third-class compartments had low partitions to the great delight of school-children. All had spoked wheels which gave them an early Victorian, not to say spidery, appearance.

These antique coaches which formed the majority of steam-hauled trains until the mid-1950s were not unpopular with all patrons. As mentioned above, school-children took great delight in travelling in third-class compartments and in being able to throw missiles over the low partitions at unsuspecting passengers in neighbouring compartments. Boys enjoyed clambering over the partitions in pursuit of each other, especially if girls were on the other side. The gas-lights in many of the 'six-wheelers' were also unreliable and gave rise to much fun and games. These lights could fade out

View of suburban train from house window in Ranelagh

when the gas was exhausted or when the accumulated rainwater trapped within the bowl surrounding the gas-light swayed so violently in the rocking carriage that it extinguished the light when the train gathered speed.

Harcourt Street Station was ideally located to serve children attending a range of different educational establishments. Almost directly opposite the station was the well-known college 'The High School' while in adjoining Adelaide Road was the Church of Ireland Diocesan School. Just off the nearby South Circular Road was the very large Christian Brothers' School in Synge Street. Also within easy walking distance of the station were the Catholic University School in Lower Leeson Street, Loreto College and Wesley College in St Stephen's Green and Alexandra College in Earlsfort Terrace. To crown the list, University College Dublin was also located in Earlsfort Terrace during the 1950s in the fine building that now houses the National Concert Hall.

Fresh Fish

Seán Ó Cinnéide worked as a fireman
on the Harcourt Street Line

To ensure that fare-paying passengers would not have to endure any unpleasant smells on their journey, it was forbidden to carry fresh fish on passenger trains. However, this did not prevent an enterprising Dublin fishmonger, known as Bid from Charlemont Street, from bringing her large three-wheeled fish basket onto the first morning train from Harcourt Street every Friday to sell her fish in Bray. Seán Ó Cinnéide, who worked as a fireman on the Harcourt Street Line in the 1950s, tells of being sent by his engine driver at the end of the journey to enquire of the guard if the woman he was seeing being helped off the train with the large three-wheeled basket was in fact carrying fresh fish. When Bid saw the fireman coming, she said to the guard 'Ah sure we'll send a few herrings up to the driver as well!' With that she handed Seán some herrings which he promptly delivered to his driver.

'Right', said the driver as he moved the engine off to the turntable, 'Now you wash that shovel there, pour water on it from the boiler, put the herrings in the water and push the shovel in over the fire for five seconds'. When that was done, the herrings were turned over and given a further five seconds in the fire. 'I've never tasted nicer fish for my breakfast,' said Seán Ó Cinnéide, 'and every day afterwards whenever that good woman travelled with us on the Harcourt Street Line she gave us our fish breakfast!'

COMMUTERS

Naturally school children and college students formed a good proportion of the regular commuters on the trains, but there were also civil servants, office workers, shop assistants and professional people. Retired railway workers recall that over the years on the Harcourt Street Line the same people would continue to appear, first school-going then to college, later to office or business and later still, when married and settled down along the line, sending their own children to school by train. Following the commuters

Steam train departing for Bray from Stillorgan

of the morning 'rush-hour' from 8.30 to 9.30am would come housekeepers from the many suburban residences to do their special shopping in the city. They would 'take the train to town' usually after 9.30am joining the less hurried professionals. As late as the 1950s many of the latter, travelling first-class of course, would not reach Harcourt Street until 10am and some were still dressed in pin-striped suits with bowler hats and rolled umbrellas, sporting a rosebud in their button-hole in summertime. Greeting them all was Mrs Maggie McLoughlin from York Street who sold newspapers at Harcourt Street station for thirty-nine years until the trains were withdrawn in 1958.

Former regular users of the Harcourt Street Line recall that the passenger flow resembled a social stepladder. The earliest morning travellers were labourers and tradesmen followed by school-children and students, then housekeepers, the professional people and finally the wealthy housewives who merely 'went to Grafton Street to have coffee in Bewley's and have a look in the shops', or the more ordinary people who 'went to Camden Street to get the messages in town'. It should be remembered that, in the 1950s, modern supermarkets had not yet developed and almost all of the day-to-day shopping was done in small local grocers' shops, which often delivered the groceries to the larger houses. Only when something special was needed would it be necessary 'to go to town'. Many of the former Bray patrons of the line remember with great regret the 8.50am 'Express' in the morning that reached Harcourt

'Evening Express' arriving in Stillorgan in 1955

Street just after 9.10am allowing them to be at their workplace well before the normal starting time of half nine. A special tram used to meet the 8.10 a.m., 8.30 a.m. and 8.50 a.m. trains on arrival at Harcourt Street to bring commuters to the city centre, until the tram service ceased in 1948. They also remember the former 5.00pm 'Evening Express' from Harcourt Street with the first stop at Stillorgan eleven minutes later. Despite all the progress since 1958, such rapid travel is no longer possible for Bray and Stillorgan commuters.

Punctuality

Mrs Kathleen Delap travelled daily by train from Carrickmines to Harcourt Street to attend Alexandra College, but her two younger sisters travelled from the same station in the opposite direction to attend The French School in Bray. To reach the station more quickly from their home on the Brennanstown Road, the girls had to cross three fields along an old Mass Path. Mrs Delap remembers distinctly that her father, a family solicitor, had *The Irish Times* delivered to Carrickmines station each morning so that he could collect it there and read his newspaper in comfort in the first class compartment on his way to work. All school children, including Kathleen Delap, travelled third class on the same train which departed promptly at 8.44am.

Her younger sisters, who travelled a little later in the opposite direction on the 9.07am from Carrickmines to Bray, were not conditioned to the punctuality required of Dublin passengers and tended to stroll along the Mass Path to the station, frequently not arriving before the train's official departure time. If the girls were not on the platform when the 9.07am arrived from Harcourt Street, the driver invariably would give two short blasts of the engine's whistle to warn the girls of their need to hurry. The train would then rest at Carrickmines – often up to five minutes – until the two sisters had arrived and then depart with a sharp reprimanding whistle. As Mrs Delap recalls, punctuality in the mornings was paramount on trains travelling north to Dublin, but for those going south to Bray the priority was to ensure that all regular passengers did not miss their train to school or to work.

The Hat Box

On the Harcourt Street Line staff communication between stations was mainly by the dedicated railway telephone system by which each signal cabin could telephone to the next nearest cabin on a telephone instrument activated by rapidly turning a handle attached to it. If a message were to be sent from Harcourt Street to Bray, it would be passed by railway telephone first to Dundrum signal cabin, from there to Foxrock cabin, from there to Shanganagh Junction cabin and finally to Bray signal cabin.

There is a story told about a lady passenger travelling from Wexford to Dundrum who inadvertently left her hat box behind on a platform seat in Wexford. When she discovered her loss on arrival in Dundrum, she was very distressed and told the Station Master her tale of woe. He quickly reassured her that he would immediately have a message telephoned to Wexford station to send the hat box urgently on to Dundrum by the earliest available train. He then instructed the Signalman at Dundrum to telephone that message down the line to Wexford, confident that the mislaid hat box would arrive within a day.

The following day, to his astonishment, a horse-box arrived in Dundrum from Wexford with an affixed label that read 'URGENT-DUNDRUM'.

DAY-TRIPPERS

For many families living in Dublin in the 1950s the Harcourt Street Line provided a wonderful outlet to the seaside for a day-trip during the summer holidays. On one Sunday 10 July 1955 over 4,000 people travelled by train from Harcourt Street Station to the seaside. It was on such occasions that scenes of near-pandemonium were witnessed at Bray station during fine summer weekends as hundreds thronged in to find their return trains. This extract from the recollections of the late J. P. O'Dea paints the scene:

> As evening wears on, returning families crowd the station and as fast as the trains leave the platform seems to fill again. Those who came to Bray to 'do the *bona fide*' (to claim entry to a pub on a Sunday on grounds of having travelled at least five miles outside the city boundary) can easily be identified, mostly by the brown-paper bags they carry but others who carry their supply interiorly by other indications. The whole place becomes a hive of activity and any extra trains complicate an already crowded situation. This evening there is an excursion from Banagher and a mystery trip from Maryborough (now Portlaoise). They will have to be fitted into the intense traffic… There is relief when they are gone and things get back to their normal state of complexity.

There is also an amusing reference to the regular practice at Bray on such occasions for dealing with the 'hard chaws' from Dublin who had too much to drink:

Heavy summer Sunday
train pulling out from Bray

Our engine is a J15 class 0-6-0 blowing off as it backs onto the train. It is evidently in
good form and so are a few convivial souls, their voices raised in song, their paper bags
tightly clutched, who are shepherded into one of the last carriages. This usual last-
minute rush delays our departure and we pull away at 10.03p.m.

Other pleasant outlets of escape from the drudgery of city life in the 1950s were the
'Dance Excursion' to the Arcadia Ballroom in Bray and the 'Sea Breeze' Excursion to
Wicklow and Arklow. It is difficult to comprehend at the beginning of the twenty-first
century what excitement attached to travelling by train to Bray for a romantic evening
in the 1950s. Hundreds availed of the dance excursions and the convenience of the old
Arcadia Ballroom just across the road from the main entrance to Bray station added to
the attraction. No doubt the unreliable gas-lighting of the old carriages was also a
further attraction. All-in tickets for both rail travel and entrance to the dance were sold
at Harcourt Street, Ranelagh, Milltown and Dundrum stations and the newspaper
advertisements proclaimed that 'books of tickets for raffle may be handed in at all
stations on night of dance'.

RATHFARNHAM AND BELGROVE FOOTBALL CLUBS

TRAIN EXCURSION
DANCE
ARCADIA BALLROOM
Friday Next

Special trains leaving Amiens Street and Harcourt St Stations at 7.25 p.m. stopping at Westland Row, Blackrock, Dun Laoire, Ranelagh Milltown and Dundrum Returning 12.30 All-in tickets (rail and dance) 6/- obtainable at above stations on night of dance

DANCING 8-12

CHICK SMITH and his ORCHESTRA

ADMISSION 4/-

BOOKS OF TICKETS FOR RAFFLE MAY BE HANDED IN AT ALL STATIONS ON NIGHT OF DANCE.

Advertisement for 'Dance Excursion' to Bray

Guardian of Morality

Dick Flynn, as a young university student and later as an accountant, was a regular traveller on the Harcourt Street Line in the 1940s and 1950s. He has fond memories of a tall and well-respected Ticket Checker, Joe Hurley, who performed a very fine public service over and above his call of duty. When working on late night Drumm trains from Harcourt Street checking the tickets, Joe Hurley would remain in the vestibule at the end of the carriage and peer through the oval window in the sliding door observing passengers 'who may have had a little too much to drink or might be inclined to some form of immoral behaviour'.

One night when Dick Flynn was travelling on the last train from Harcourt Street to Bray, an inebriated passenger sat in front of him and began to jeer him for wearing a 'Pioneer Pin', an emblem signifying abstinence from alcoholic drink. The drunkard persisted with much loud and annoying talk, but as the train reached Ranelagh the sliding door of the vestibule opened and the 'Guardian of Morality', Joe Hurley, appeared. The drunkard fumbled and searched his pockets in vain for his ticket. 'Where are you going?' asked the Ticket Checker. 'Bray' came the muffled reply. 'I'll come back to you' said the Ticket Checker and

proceeded through the train. When he returned, the drunkard was again castigating Dick Flynn. 'Where's your ticket?' demanded the Checker and, as the train pulled out of Milltown, the drunkard fumbled again. 'You have had plenty of talk but no ticket. You either pay up now or get off!'

As there was no reaction from the drunkard, the Checker marched him down the centre of the carriage and out on to the platform at the next station, Dundrum. When Dick Flynn reached his destination at Bray, imagine his surprise when he noticed the Ticket Checker going to the Guard's Van, unlocking it and releasing the crestfallen drunkard.

The threat of being put off the train by Ticket Checker Joe Hurley was a strong deterrent to any passenger misbehaving on the Harcourt Street Line. It was also reassuring to parents of younger passengers that the Ticket Checker maintained a watchful eye from the vestibule window on people suspected of annoying or even molesting vulnerable passengers. Thanks to that fine public spirit of Ticket Checkers like Joe Hurley, travel on late night trains on the Harcourt Street Line was much safer than it is today.

Ranelagh station was also well-used for travelling out of the city suburbs. Many of the older residents associated the Harcourt Street Line with going to the sea at Shankill for a summer swim or going to Bray for a week's holiday every summer. Only the very privileged would go for a fortnight's holiday; the average Dubliner in the 1950s would just take a few day-trips during the annual holidays in the summer months. Carrickmines and Shankill were popular destinations as they were good starting points for walks into the hills towards Carrickgollogan and the Scalp or to the chimney of the disused lead works on top of Ballycorus Hill. The country lanes around Carrickmines were thick with blackberry bushes and were a favourite haunt of whole families picking blackberries every autumn. Shankill station was also the starting point of a pleasant walk to the sea across the old Dublin-Bray main road, along tree-shaded Corbawn Lane, across the bridge over the coastal railway line (where Shankill DART station is now located) and down the cliffs to the shingle beach at Shanganagh for a swim.

Much of the regular traffic for Milltown station was provided by nearby university hostels but by far the most used station all the year round was Dundrum. It catered on a daily basis for large numbers of city-bound commuters as well as those travelling to Dundrum to work in nearby houses, shops or farms. The volume of traffic at Dundrum was sufficient to support a well-stocked bookstall on the Dublin platform, which was staffed by a Ms Pogue in the final years of the line. The only other bookstalls on the line were at Harcourt Street and Bray stations.

Foxrock station for many older Dubliners brings back great memories of days spent at Leopardstown Races. Long special trains of usually older six-wheeled carriages were provided from Harcourt Street on race days and stored on the spacious sidings at Foxrock while racing was in progress. The smoke and steam rising from these waiting trains provided the usual backdrop to the racecourse when viewed from the stands in railway days. Former patrons who travelled by train to Leopardstown Races recall the real excitement at Foxrock station on race days with horse-box wagons being shunted to various sidings and dense crowds of race-goers hurrying across both the tracks and the long station bridge that led to ticket-booths on the special race platform. Rose Mary Daly in her research of the Harcourt Street Line found that at one time rail traffic was considerable on race days, particularly the St Stephen's Day meeting just after Christmas. She instances one particularly wet day 8 March 1941 when Harcourt Street trains brought 719 first class passengers and 2,666 third class passengers to the Leopardstown Races.

▲ Race-goers alighting from 'Race Special' at Foxrock

◄ Lunchtime train about to leave Foxrock

Leopardstown Race Course in the 1950s. The paths at the bottom of the picture lead to Foxrock station

Leopardstown Races

Horse racing at Leopardstown, right beside Foxrock station, provided the heaviest traffic for the Harcourt Street Line. Race meetings were held about once a month, usually on Saturday afternoons although some Friday evening meetings were held from the mid 1950s. To cater for the additional traffic there were normally two 'Race Specials', supplemented by extra coaches on the regular trains. Rakes of ancient and little-used six-wheelers, stored both at Harcourt Street and Foxrock stations, were brought into service for the 'Race Specials' and stories abound on their extraordinary condition. Birds' nests were found in the roofs of some of these nineteenth-century carriages and, in order to provide extra first class accommodation, CIÉ posted strips of the white paper rolls used for bus tickets over the figure '3' on the outside of third class compartment doors!

The St Stephen's Day meeting attracted the largest and most important crowd of the year. For that meeting four 'Race Specials' were run providing quite a busy schedule, as may be seen from Appendix 2 for 26 December 1953. In the steam era, double-heading of 'Race Specials' was common and larger than normal engines were used, such as former Great Southern & Western D4 4-4-0 loco 335 and former Great Southern Railways J15b 0-6-0 locos 717 and 718. A clear indication of the Leopardstown Races was seen at Harcourt Street on mornings of race meetings in the sight of dozens of loud-voiced hawkers of all descriptions descending on the station and clamouring to get into the guard's van of the regular suburban trains with their three-wheeled wicker tubs filled to the brim with fruit and confectionary to be sold later in the day to race-goers as they descended from the 'Race Specials' at Foxrock.

Foxrock station was also the terminus of a number of suburban trains on the Harcourt Street-Bray route, most notably the 1.10pm 'lunchtime train' which returned from Foxrock at 2.10pm. In the more leisurely days of the 1950s this train – usually comprising one composite coach with separate first-class, third-class and guard compartments – allowed many office workers and civil servants ample time to travel home for their lunch-break and be back at work within the one and a half hours allowed. Life at that time was much more leisurely than nowadays and this is evidenced in the train timetables of the 1950s. The morning 'rush hour' extended from 8am to 9am at Bray with four trains departing for Harcourt Street, the principal train being the 8.52am 'Express' which reached the city terminus in 23 minutes, with one compulsory stop at Ranelagh. The evening 'rush hour' at Harcourt Street stretched from 5pm to 6.10pm with four departures, the principal train being the 5pm 'Evening Express', initially with its first stop at Stillorgan reached in 12 minutes, and later with Dundrum as first stop reached in a mere 7 minutes. Apart from the half-hourly 'rush hour' service, trains ran roughly at hourly intervals during the day on the Harcourt Street Line stopping at all stations and completing the twelve mile journey in 33 minutes.

CHANGE FROM STEAM TO DIESEL

During the 1950s the Harcourt Street Line began losing money heavily, largely due to its out-of–town terminus, its many ill-sited stations and the development of bus routes from suburbs directly into the city centre. Faced with this problem, CIÉ decided first to improve the standard of the steam-hauled trains and then to introduce a number of diesel railcars in an effort to improve the viability of the railway. As new carriages were acquired for CIÉ mainline services the older pre-war corridor carriages were released for use on other services including the Harcourt Street Line. These were 'bogie' coaches, with a four-wheeled bogie at each end of the long carriage giving a much more comfortable ride than the old 'six-wheelers' which were gradually relegated to special excursions, 'Race Specials' or to supplementary seaside trains at week-ends.

By 1955 six-wheeled carriages had almost disappeared from regular Harcourt-Bray steam-hauled trains and a number of diesel railcars had been introduced to replace steam trains at off-peak hours. Many of the photographs reproduced in this book reflect this period in the mid-1950s as the gradual transition from steam to diesel trains was taking place. By April 1956 three railcar sets were operating on the Harcourt Street Line

Old six-wheelers on 'Race Special' passing Stillorgan

and only two steam trains daily in each direction remained compared with twenty diesel trains. On 24 June 1957 the large steam engine shed at Bray was turned over to diesel motive power, effectively ending steam operation. The Harcourt Street Line was henceforth operated almost exclusively by diesel railcars, the only exception being the Rosslare mainline trains some of which ran from Harcourt Street during the summer months hauled by an A class diesel locomotive. The popular 'Sea Breeze' excursion on Wednesdays and Saturdays to Wicklow and Arklow, formed usually of a rake of old 'six-wheelers' hauled by one or two steam engines, was replaced by a train of more modern 'bogie' coaches and from 11 August 1956 was hauled by a modern A class diesel engine. Even the notorious rake of old nineteenth-century carriages (one of which carried a builder's plate dated 1875), which had been used to convey race-goers to Leopardstown Race Meetings, was replaced by a modern six-coach diesel railcar set.

The introduction of diesel railcars and locomotives to the Harcourt Street Line brought about some acceleration in the train services. The times taken by stopping trains to traverse the twelve miles to and from Bray were generally cut from 33 to 30 minutes and the 8.50am 'Express' with one stop at Ranelagh had a new 20 minute schedule to Harcourt Street instead of the previous 23 minutes. In 1957 Shanganagh Junction was relayed with new tracks that also helped faster running. By this time, however, a large number of previously loyal patrons had forsaken the Harcourt Street Line. Because of the poor standard of trains and timings throughout the early and mid-

Large steam engine shed at Bray before closure in 1957

Lower O'Connell Street in the 1950s with D'Olier Street visible at top left

1950s, many patrons had been driven to seek more reliable public transport. This they found in the more frequent bus services continually being developed by CIÉ during the final years of the line.

Since the summer of 1956, CIÉ had been quietly developing a policy that sought to cope with all demands for public transport in the South Dublin suburbs by expanding its city bus services. While not curtailing any Harcourt Street Line services, CIÉ began to publicise competing bus services and even introduced a special service of unlimited buses from D'Olier Street in the centre of Dublin direct to the stands at Leopardstown Race Course in competition with its own special train service. Unlike the bus passengers, rail travellers to Foxrock station would find themselves about half a mile away from the stands.

Another glaring example of its obvious policy to minimise the potential of the Harcourt Street Line also occurred in 1956. Since the Second World War CIÉ had resisted restoring the pre-war Sunday services on Dublin suburban lines for any period other than the summer months extending from Whit Sunday to mid-September. In May 1956, however, CIÉ announced to a storm of protest from Bray traders that Sunday trains on the Dublin Suburban lines would operate only on Whit Sunday 21 May and from 1 July to 26 August inclusive. Despite numerous representations from local organisations calling for a train service to Bray in June, CIÉ publicly stated that their buses could cope satisfactorily with any traffic offering. This contention was disproved emphatically on Sunday 10 June when fine weather attracted Dubliners in their thousands to the seaside. Although it was estimated that 70 buses an hour left the city for the Dún Laoghaire direction and a further 30 an hour for Bray, long queues formed faster than they could be got away. No doubt because of these chaotic conditions CIÉ announced that the train service to Bray would commence from the following Sunday 17 June and continue until mid-September. This, perhaps, was the most striking evidence of CIÉ's determination to try and prove that suburban rail routes like the Harcourt Street Line were no longer needed. But it also provided striking evidence of the inability of road services to cater for heavy passenger movements that ideally suited the railways.

CHAPTER 8

Character of the Old Line

A trip on the Harcourt Street Line began in an atmosphere of expectancy. Passengers entered the terminus between Doric columns on each side of a high arched entrance inscribed with Roman numerals giving the opening date MDCCCLIX (1859). The imposing colonnaded terminus, designed by the railway architect George Wilkinson, still stands at the top of Harcourt Street as a protected building and contains The Odeon Bar & Restaurant at street level and The POD Bar and Nightclub at ground level.

On entering the Main Hall of the building the prospective railway traveller found a spacious station refreshment room and bar to the left and ticket booking offices to the right. From the Main Hall two fine curved stone stairways ascended in opposite directions to a single 200m station platform some 9m above street level. This platform, covered for only half its length, was an anti-climax for a first-time traveller who expected much more after the impressive station entrance. Indeed the terminus was described as magnificent on the outside until you get to the inside. Dubliners referred to it as an egg – 'a lovely shell on the outside with just a yolk inside'. Schoolchildren of the 1950s will remember its single platform as the exception to the teacher's rule that there were two sides to every story – 'except Harcourt Street Station!'

Yet despite all the jibes and jokes, Harcourt Street Station was one of Dublin's mainline terminals for over 90 years until 1953 serving the entire South-East as far as Wexford, Rosslare and Waterford. For many years it was a busy station handling up to 30 suburban trains a day to Foxrock, Bray and Greystones; mainline passenger and goods trains to the South-East; and many excursion trains including the 'Sea Breeze' excursions to Wicklow and Arklow; 'Dance Excursion' trains to Bray and 'Race Specials' to Leopardstown Race Meetings.

Live Calves in Sacks

In the regulations governing the carriage of passengers by rail it was forbidden to convey goods, other than parcels, by passenger trains. All goods had to be forwarded to their destination by designated goods trains.

As the Harcourt Street Line did not have designated goods trains since the mid-1920s, ways and means had to be found to get around the regulations in order to send urgent goods to their destination. The ingenious solution devised was to forward live chickens, live poultry and even live young cattle on passenger trains as 'parcels'. Jim Dowling, who travelled daily by train from Dundrum to school and university in Dublin, remembers vividly seeing the extraordinary sight on the opposite Bray platform of heads of live calves sticking out of sacks in the mornings as he waited for his train to school. These sacks would be loaded into the guard's van of the 8.45am passenger train to Bray, where they would then be transferred onwards to the south-east by the following Harcourt Street-Wexford mainline train which did not stop at Dundrum.

Jim Dowling, at right with his brother Pat, travelled daily from Dundrum to school and university

The extensive trackwork of the station bore witness to earlier times when considerable goods traffic was handled in addition to passenger trains. Midway along the single platform stood a massive water-tank with a capacity of 12,750 gallons to service the steam engines, while east of the platform lay a large goods shed (leased in later years to Dunlop Tyres) and extensive sidings used for storing engines and carriages. Goods wagons were still in evidence on these sidings up to 1950 when regular 'mixed' passenger and goods trains ceased on the Harcourt Street Line. Mail and parcels traffic handled after 1950 were hoisted to platform level by lift from a large yard with a double-gate entrance from Harcourt Street.

A most unusual feature of the station was that the mainline from the south-east terminated on a 15m turntable in a roofless area situated at the end of the single platform just before the buffer stops. This turntable allowed engines of incoming trains, on being released from their carriages, to be turned around to face towards Bray and

▲ Exterior of Harcourt Street Station today

◀ Station interior in 1958

run around the carriages on a parallel track to rejoin the train at the outer end. The ceremony of 'turning the engine' was one that delighted all children coming off the incoming trains. They used to rush to the end of the platform to stand in awe and watch the hissing steam monster being miraculously turned around in less than two minutes by only two men pushing the finely-balanced turntable.

The origin of Harcourt Street station may be traced to a proposal in 1846 to build an inland route to Bray in opposition to the pioneer Dublin & Kingstown Railway that aspired to extend its coastal line to Bray via Dalkey. Two separate companies were involved in the inland route – The Dublin Dundrum & Rathfarnham Railway and the Waterford Wexford Wicklow & Dublin Railway. Their lines were to meet in Dundrum but in the event a new and less ambitious company – The Dublin & Wicklow Railway – built the Bray-Dundrum section and then took over the other company's line from Dublin. The opening of the line took place to a temporary terminus at Harcourt Road in 1854 but the railway was extended to the Harcourt Street terminal in 1859.

▲ Engine being turned on
Harcourt Street turntable

▶ View of turntable and
buffer stop at Harcourt Street
Station (The Round End' in
Beckett's *Watt*)

▲ Diesel train at platform about to depart

◀ Steam train arriving at Ranelagh in 1955

THREE MILES TO DUNDRUM

On departure from Harcourt Street Station, even before reaching the end of the platform, passengers could look out over the ornamental cast-iron parapet of the wide bridge over Harcourt Road and on their right could see up along the South Circular Road as far as Leonard's Corner. Having passed the signal cabin and the former engine shed on their left, the single line from the platform became double-track and the train soon crossed the Grand Canal by a three-span bridge over Charlemont Mall, the Canal and Grand Parade. It then proceeded along a massive stone-faced embankment crossing in succession Dartmouth, Northbrook, Ranelagh and Charleston Roads before arriving at the first station situated partly on a bridge over Dunville Avenue. It is a tribute to the nineteenth-century builders of the original route from Grand Parade that this same embankment is again being used in the twenty-first century to carry the new Luas from Sandyford to St Stephen's Green.

Although its official name appeared as *Rathmines & Ranelagh / Ráth Maoinis agus Raghnallaigh*, this first halt just one mile from Harcourt Street in a built-up suburban area was always referred to by the public and staff alike simply as Ranelagh. In 1958 when the line was closed this station had the distinction of being under the control of

Arklow train passing Milltown
at speed in 1955

a Haltmistress, Miss Daly, instead of the normal Station Master. Reached by long flights of wooden stairs from Dunville Avenue, it was not an imposing station having partly-wooden platforms and low corrugated-iron buildings. Yet it did serve a most important function in the operation of the Harcourt Street Line. Following the sensational accident at Harcourt Street station on St Valentine's Day 1900 when a cattle train from Enniscorthy failed to stop and crashed through the buffer-stops, it became obligatory for all trains travelling to Dublin to stop at Ranelagh and then proceed with caution towards Harcourt Street.

Beyond Ranelagh the train climbed continuously passing under footbridges at Upper Beechmount Avenue and Cowper Road until the station named *Milltown / Baile an Mhuilinn* was reached 1.75 miles from Harcourt Street in a very quiet suburb. Milltown was notable in latter years as the station run by two ladies, the Misses Murphy, both of whom wore dark blue shop coats. Just beyond the station was the largest civil

▲ 1948 Winter Timetable cover

◀ Diesel railcar train crossing the Nine Arches in 1956

engineering feature of the line, a magnificent nine-arch stone viaduct that today carries Luas over the Dodder River Valley. This viaduct, constructed with rectangular cut blocks of limestone, is a substantial memorial to the skills of the nineteenth-century engineers and stone masons. CIÉ was so proud of this viaduct known locally as 'The Nine Arches' that it was featured on the cover of its national railway timetable for winter 1948 with the 5pm Harcourt Street-Wexford train crossing over and the tall chimney of the old Dublin Laundry at Milltown in the background. A comparison between the view on that cover and a view of the same viaduct today shows remarkably little change since 1948.

While crossing 'The Nine Arches' passengers had a view upstream towards The Dropping Well tavern and beyond it their first panoramic view of the Dublin Mountains which remained in sight for the greater part of their onward journey to Bray. Continuing to climb along this very scenic line and pass under another footbridge at Windy Arbour the train veered southwards to an embankment that ended with a short bridge over the junction of Taney Road and Dundrum Road – the site of today's magnificent cable-stayed Luas bridge. Just south of the bridge was one of the busiest and best-sited stations on the line, *Dundrum / Dún Droma*, some three miles from Harcourt Street. This fine station, with access both from the Main Street and Taney

William Dargan, Builder of the Line

Outside the National Gallery of Ireland on Merrion Street, Dublin, stands a fine statue of William Dargan, builder of the greater part of Ireland's railways including the Harcourt Street Line. He was a legend in his own lifetime, an extraordinarily successful railway contractor who devoted his great energy and fortune to raising the morale of the Irish people in the aftermath of the Great Famine 1845-1850. His financing, single-handed, of the Dublin International Exhibition in 1853 ranks him as a giant among Irish entrepreneurs.

In April 1833 Dargan was given the contract to build Ireland's first railway. Within twenty months The Dublin & Kingstown Railway was completed and opened in December 1834, placing William Dargan in the front rank of Irish public works contractors. In the following years Dargan was sought out by promoters of railway building schemes then beginning to proliferate in mid-nineteenth century Ireland. He undertook many prestigious schemes, including the Ulster Railway to Armagh, the Midland & Great Western Railway to Galway and the Great Southern & Western Railway mainline to Cork.

William Dargan was most closely associated with the building of the Harcourt Street Line, having been appointed contractor both for the Bray-Dundrum and Dublin-Dundrum sections. For his construction work he took bonds in payment, exchanging these later for shares in the Dublin & Wicklow Railway Company. He became a Director of the Company in 1856 and was chosen as Chairman in 1864. He bought Mount Anville House close to Dundrum station as his residence and farm, where he reared fine herds of sheep and cattle. Flowers from his gardens and crops, such as sugar beet, developed on his farm were famous at exhibitions. Queen Victoria, who paid an official visit to the 1853 Dublin Exhibition, also visited Mount Anville. There the queen offered William Dargan a baronetcy, but he declined the honour.

The depopulation and despair that swept the country in the wake of the Great Famine affected Dargan deeply. A severe fall from his horse early in 1866 incapacitated him at a time of great financial stress. Circumstances began to turn against him, illness grew rapidly and he died early in 1867 aged 68 years. At his funeral, hundreds of railway workers marched through Dublin to pay tribute to William Dargan, the man who saved so many from starvation by providing employment in the building of railways throughout Ireland.

Statue of William Dargan outside the National Gallery

View of Dundrum station towards Bray

Road, had a booking office on both platforms. In the 1950s it served the needs of the adjacent village, its surrounding suburban homes and the farmlands stretching as far as the Dublin Mountains.

Dundrum station, originally planned as the terminus of the line, boasted an impressive mid-Victorian single-storey building on the Taney Road side which still stands today as a protected structure. Its most recent use was as construction project office for Luas Line B. This elegant station was designed and built by William Dargan, the famous builder of the greater part of Ireland's railway system. Mr Dargan in 1851 bought the nearby Mount Anville as his farm and residence, became a Director of the Dublin & Wicklow Railway in 1856 and was chosen as its Chairman in 1864. Being such an important person, he held a season ticket for the line and regularly used Dundrum as his own local station.

For many years up to the 1950s Dundrum station was the destination of boarding students attending the well-known St Columba's College Rathfarnham over two miles

Nameboards on Dundrum station platform

away. For this reason the signal cabin on the Dublin platform carried a large sign 'Station for St Columba's College', a sign almost as large as the bi-lingual nameboard of the station itself. Dundrum catered for goods traffic by rail as well as a sizeable suburban passenger traffic. A siding on the Dublin side served businesses in the Dundrum area and was used for many purposes, including milk vans for O'Connor's Dairy, wagons of bagged cement for local builders and occasional horse boxes. It was

Dundrum Incline

Located so close to the foothills of the Dublin Mountains, Dundrum station had an air of being sited almost on an outlying spur of the hills. Looking south from the station platforms towards Stillorgan the double-track railway was seen to climb up through a deep rock cutting that continued for about two miles to reach a plateau at Lakelands, which marked the summit of the Harcourt Street Line. For trains approaching Dundrum from Stillorgan the downward gradients from Lakelands ranged from 1 in 95 to 1 in 76 to 1 in 96, steep enough to require skilful driving and control of rail vehicles.

Regular passengers recall that it was not unknown for trains coming from the south to run through the station

before being able to stop, then having to set back to the platform. On one such occasion, a lady passenger was overheard to remark 'He must be only learning'! Other rail users, who certainly were not learners, were the four-man gang of rail maintenance workers – known as platelayers – based in Dundrum. They pushed a four-wheel bogey on which they carried their maintenance equipment. A strange but familiar sight that often greeted passengers awaiting trains in the evenings was the platelayers' bogey silently coming down the incline from Stillorgan with four happy men sitting on their equipment having finished their day's work!

also used for the despatch of sugar-beet from surrounding farms destined for Carlow Sugar Factory. The last Station Master of Dundrum Mr Andrew Smith confirmed that there used to be a very heavy goods traffic up to the 1950s.

View of Stillorgan station with steam engine passing

THREE MILES TO FOXROCK

Beyond Dundrum station the character of the Harcourt Street Line changed completely. Entering a deep rock cutting and climbing steeply through an outlying spur of the Dublin Mountains, the line's original suburban pretensions gave way to those of a rural branch line with fine views over a thinly-populated countryside. After two miles the line reached its summit at Lakelands and then levelled out parallel to a large Dublin Corporation Reservoir before reaching the remote rural station of *Stillorgan / Teach Lorgán*. This station was located just over five miles from Harcourt Street at the top of Brewery Road and was over a mile from Stillorgan village. The former Station Master's house is still occupied today as a residence and is almost directly facing the Luas depot at Sandyford.

Topiary of 'Stillorgan' on Bray side platform

In the 1950s Stillorgan station generated only light traffic for the railway. The surrounding rural area did not provide many regular passengers, although some traffic was generated by the nearby Leopardstown Park Hospital for disabled soldiers and sailors of the twentieth-century World Wars, whose blue uniforms and caps with their white shirts and red ties were distinctive in the area. Stillorgan station was notable for its tidiness and topiary. The station's name was beautifully sculpted in box-hedge on the Bray side platform, adding to its neat and tidy appearance that won many prizes during the 1950s for Haltkeeper Paddy Doyle in the annual Best Kept Station Competition run by CIÉ.

Just beyond Stillorgan station the train passed under the old Brewery Road and soon crossed the old Leopardstown Road by an unusual level crossing. The gates guarding this narrow road were not wide enough to extend across the full double-track railway. This left a large and dangerous gap that allowed children, dogs and other animals to stray quite freely on to the Harcourt Street Line. In 1957 a fatal collision between two diesel railcar trains near Dundrum was caused by a stray cow on the line. Beyond the level crossing the line skirted the eastern perimeter of Leopardstown Race Course to reach the largest and most important intermediate station on the line, *Foxrock / Cúirt an Choirnéil*. Just six miles from Harcourt Street, Foxrock station was located beside the village on its left and the race course on its right, serving their needs and those of the nearby affluent houses known as the 'stockbroker belt'. The station also served workers from the surrounding agricultural area, including the staff, patrons and horses travelling to and from Leopardstown Race Course.

94

Samuel Beckett and Foxrock Station

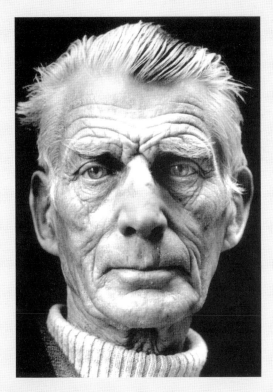

Samuel Beckett

(Excitedly, in the distance.) She's coming. (Pause. Nearer.) She's at the level-crossing! (Immediately exaggerated station sounds. Falling signals. Bells. Whistles. Crescendo of train whistle approaching. Sound of train rushing through station.)

(All That Fall, p. 27)

He was also able to describe most beautifully the pastoral elegance of his local station at Foxrock:

And so they stayed a little while, Mr Case and Mr Nolan looking at Mr Gorman and Mr Gorman looking straight before him, at nothing in particular, though the sky falling to the hills, and the hills falling to the plain, made as pretty a picture in the early morning light, as a man could hope to meet with, in a day's march.

(Watt, p. 246)

Most interestingly, Samuel Beckett was able to detect the pervasive snobbery on the affluent Harcourt Street Line:

Come, Dolly darling, let us take up our stand before the first class smokers. Give me your hand and hold me tight, one can be sucked under.

(All That Fall, p. 25)

The Harcourt Street Line was regularly used for many years by Samuel Beckett, winner of the Nobel Prize for Literature in 1969. He was born in the family home at Cooldrinagh on Brighton Road, Foxrock, not far from the station. As a young boy, student, and later lecturer at Trinity College, he used the Harcourt Street Line as his means of transport to and from Dublin. Mrs Kathleen Delap recalls that Sam Beckett was always very interested in the railway and got to know its passengers and staff so well that he wrote a radio-play *All That Fall* set in Foxrock station. He also featured the line, its characters and their eccentricities in one of his early novels *Watt*.

Samuel Beckett had a unique talent to convey the atmosphere of a railway station in his radio-play:

The Station Master at Foxrock in Beckett's time was Thomas Farrell, who became Mr Barrell in *All That Fall* and Mr Gorman in *Watt*. He was renowned for managing his station with unusual efficiency and often won first prize for the best-kept station on the line. In the radio-play, the Station Master is sarcastically ridiculed by Mrs Rooney.

Before you slink away, Mr Barrell, please, a statement of some kind, I insist. Even the slowest train on this brief line is not ten minutes and more behind its scheduled time without good cause, one imagines. (Pause.) We all know your station is the best-kept of the entire network, but there are times when that is not enough, just not enough.

Foxrock station in winter during Beckett's time

(Pause.) Now, Mr Barrell, leave off chewing your whiskers, we are waiting to hear from you – we the unfortunate ticket-holders' nearest if not dearest.

(All That Fall, pp.26-27)

In the novel *Watt*, there is an interesting episode where Watt purchases a third-class ticket at Foxrock for one shilling and three pence.

He wants a ticket to the end of the line, cried Mr Nolan.
Is it a white man? said Lady McCann.
Which end? said Mr Gorman.
What end? said Mr Nolan.
Watt did not reply.
The round end or the square end? said Mr Nolan.

(Watt, p. 244)

The round end of the line was the Harcourt Street terminus which, unlike the Bray terminus, ended on a turntable.

▲ Diploma won by Foxrock Station Master Myles Doyle

View of Foxrock station towards Dublin

Diesel 'Race Special' beside finely-shaped hedges in 1958

Foxrock station was extensive. As well as the main platforms, a special third platform was provided for trains to race meetings and all the platforms were connected by a long iron footbridge spanning the width of the station. The race platform had booths selling entrance tickets and race cards as well as special turnstiles giving direct access to the race course. The former station entrance to the course still survives today beside the imposing gateway to Leopardstown Golf Centre. North and south of Foxrock station were storage sidings for 'Race Specials' while adjoining the main station building on the site now occupied by the 'Hedgerows' modern housing scheme was a further siding to handle goods traffic and horse-boxes.

Foxrock station was renowned for its flowering shrubs and finely-shaped hedges. Deservedly, for six consecutive years from 1947, it won first prize for Station Master Myles Doyle for the Best Kept Station in the Dublin Region. This tradition was continued right up to the closure of the line by his successor Mr McHale and Foreman Joe Hart. The main platforms here as at all intermediate stations on the line displayed large bi-lingual nameboards. Interestingly at this station the name of the nearby village

Drivers and firemen who worked trains to Bray from Harcourt Street and Amiens Street stations (Seán Ó Cinnéide is third from left)

of Foxrock was shown in English, but the Irish name was Cúirt an Choirnéil referring to the townland of Cornelscourt which later became well-known as the location of the first large supermarket in south county Dublin. Strangely the name Cúirt an Choirnéil was not featured on the bi-lingual railway tickets used on the Harcourt Street Line. The Irish name shown on the tickets was Carraig an tSionnaigh.

It is worthy of note that Foxrock is the only former Harcourt Street Line station that is not planned to be served by Luas in the foreseeable future. Due to the low density and obvious affluence of the population around Foxrock village today, Luas planners have responded to public demand in deciding eventually to extend Line B further to the west of Foxrock by way of Ballyogan through an area where extensive housing development is planned. Should this extension of Luas be built it would be intended to serve Leopardstown race course at its eastern end towards Carrickmines.

Carrickmines station with its water tank

THREE MILES TO SHANKILL

Beyond Foxrock the Harcourt Street Line began its descent towards the coast at Bray. Skirting the race course on the right and many luxurious homes on the left, the train passed through good agricultural land and approached another remote station *Carrickmines / Carraig Mhaighin* seven miles from Harcourt Street. This station in latter years was managed by a Haltmistress, Miss Brisley, and was located near Carrickmines Croquet & Lawn Tennis Club at an over-bridge on the Glenamuck Road about one-and-a-half miles from the village of Kiltiernan. The only unusual feature of the station was its large water tank with a capacity of 6,800 gallons to replenish the steam engines from 'Race Specials' run to Foxrock on days of Leopardstown race meetings.

On leaving Carrickmines the train resumed its descent towards the sea, passing Barrington Tower on the left at the top of Glendruid and traversing beautiful scenery of rich farmlands. It then whistled past Tully Gates, a rural level crossing with a strange two-armed signal, and gave a glimpse on the right of the ancient Christian church and crosses of Tully, first mentioned in the fifteenth-century Book of Lismore. The train then reached the second major engineering feature of the line known as 'The Bride's Glen Viaduct'. This magnificent five-arch granite stone structure carried the Harcourt

View of Shankill station towards Bray

Shankill Shunting

Jim Kiernan, who was attached to Bray Locomotive Shed during the 1950s, rose through the ranks from Engine Cleaner to Engine Driver and has a wealth of information on the detailed workings of the Harcourt Street Line. During his time there were 100 ground staff employed by the Locomotive Department in Bray, as well as 34 drivers and 34 firemen rostered for both the Harcourt Street and Amiens Street lines. He speaks with pride of the great camaraderie that existed between the railway staff in Bray, many of whom were known only by their nicknames.

In the early 1950s, Jim was working as a fireman on the Bray Pilot Engine – former Midland & Great Western G2 2-4-0 loco 657 – and the crew was responsible for working occasional goods wagons from Bray to Shankill, in order to avoid shunting the 'mixed' afternoon train to Harcourt Street at a station situated on an incline descending all the way to Bray. One day he and his driver received instructions to collect a 'hard head' goods wagon from the siding in

Shankill. They departed from Bray, accompanied by the Porter/Shunter who was affectionately known as 'Porky' Nolan.

Having reached Shankill the loco reversed across the trailing crossover to enter the siding off the down road, collected the wagon and left it alongside the down platform, with the intention of returning to the up road and running around the wagon before hauling it to Bray. However, when the wagon was unhooked from the loco, the crew noticed to their horror that the wagon had started to move down the track. Assuming that the wagon's brake blocks were badly worn, they shouted to 'Porky' to apply the wagon's hand brake. He did so at once, but to no avail. So 'Porky' decided to jump up on the brake handle to apply the pressure of his whole body to the hand brake. But in spite of this brave action, he failed to halt the wagon and it continued to gather speed. With 'Porky' still standing on the brake handle and desperately clutching on to its side,

Engine No. 462 shunting wagons at Foxrock

the runaway wagon passed the length of the down platform and headed off down the mainline towards Shanganagh Junction.

The signalman at Shankill immediately telephoned his counterpart at Shanganagh to warn him of the incident and to make sure the road through the junction was clear for the runaway wagon. Shortly afterwards the signalman at Shanganagh saw a solitary wagon come rumbling past with poor 'Porky' still on the brake handle and clinging on to the wagon for dear life. Shanganagh then telephoned Bray Cabin urgently requesting that the level crossing gates be opened for the runaway wagon and that all efforts be made to stop it alongside the down platform. Very soon, people waiting at the level crossing in Bray for an expected train to pass saw only the extraordinary sight of this wagon passing them with the Porter/Shunter still clinging on to it for dear life. In fact, the wagon could not be stopped in the station and the signalman finally directed it past Bray Shed and off the mainline into the lower-level carriage storage area with a slightly rising gradient, known locally as 'The Wicklow Sidings'. There the runaway wagon finally ground to a halt having travelled well over three miles from Shankill with poor 'Porky' Nolan desperately clutching on to its side!

Street Line over the deep valley of the Loughlinstown River. It may still be admired to this day high above Cherrywood Road some distance behind St Colmcille's Hospital, Loughlinstown. Having crossed the viaduct the train passed the Paupers' Burial Ground containing the remains of victims of the Great Famine of 1845-1850. It then passed under Stonebridge Road to reach the last intermediate station on the line *Shankill / Seinchill.*

Located almost ten miles from Harcourt Street this station was just off the Dublin Road opposite St Anne's Church at the end of a short road appropriately named Station Road. It served the nearby village of Shankill as well as the rural communities of Rathmichael and Shanganagh. Behind the platform on the Bray side was a special siding

Steam train passing
Woodbrook golf halt

originally built to serve the Ballycorus lead works. It was used up to the end of the nineteenth century to receive ore from Glendasan in Co Wicklow, which was carted to Rathdrum and then sent by rail to Shankill, from where it was again carted to the smelting works at Ballycorus over two miles away. The old chimney of the lead works can still be seen on top of the nearby hills. In later years the siding was used for local goods traffic and horse boxes. The last Station Master at Shankill, Mr Delaney, bought the station house as a residence and some years after the line was closed sold it as a business premises. The former station building survives today as 'Station House' and is part of the Shankill Business Centre.

THREE MILES TO BRAY

South of Shankill station the line passed under the old Dublin-Bray main road and curved in a long arc for about a mile to Shanganagh Junction, where the double tracks of the Harcourt Street Line joined those of the Dublin-Bray coastal line some two miles north of Bray. No station existed at Shanganagh Junction, only a signal cabin that controlled both routes as they converged on Bray. The combined lines continued their descent passing through Woodbrook Golf Club where a special railway halt existed to facilitate golfers. Finally the lines crossed the Dargle River at Bray Harbour on a three-span iron bridge and swung south past Bray Gas Works into the spacious station of *Bray / Brí Chualann*.

Busy summer week-end scene at Bray with three tracks occupied

Bray was the terminus of most Harcourt Street Line trains, although five of the 23 weekday trains in the final years were extended to Greystones. Many of the other trains made a connection at Bray with trains from the Amiens Street-Bray coastal line that were running through to Greystones. To cater for services on both routes to Dublin the layout of Bray station provided a central third track between the platform tracks on each side of the station. Arrivals and departures for Harcourt Street normally used the seaward platform, while those for the coastal route normally used the main platform nearest the town. The central track was used to allow engines to run around their trains in preparation for the return trip to Dublin. When Bray station served both suburban routes to Dublin up to the end of 1958, it often presented a very busy scene especially at rush hour and during summer weekends when thousands of day-trippers travelled by train to Bray.

Passengers awaiting Dublin-bound train at Stillorgan station

CHAPTER 9

Drumm Trains

· ·

Drumm train D at Bray

For a period of seventeen years, from 1932 to 1949, passengers on the Harcourt Street Line enjoyed the efficient operation of electric railcars popularly known as the 'Drumm Trains'. These trains drew their power from batteries stored underneath the coaches rather than from an overhead wire system as used by DART and Luas railcars. The four battery-operated trains derived their name from Dr James Drumm and his team at University College Dublin (UCD), who developed industrial-sized rechargeable batteries powerful enough to drive a two-coach articulated railcar at speeds of 45 mph.

Following the opening of the State's first hydro-electric generating station at Ardnacrusha in 1929, the government was anxious to encourage industries to consume electric power. It saw an opportunity for using electricity to revitalise the Irish railway system within the State and provided UCD with finance to assess the potential of the rechargeable Drumm batteries for this purpose. An existing Drewry four-wheel petrol-driven railcar was converted to battery operation by the Great Southern Railways (GSR) – precursor to Córas Iompair Éireann (CIÉ) – and tested satisfactorily on the Dublin-Cork mainline. In 1930 the GSR was authorised by the government to construct a full-sized two-coach train powered by two 300hp 600 volt direct current motors driving axles of the central bogies. The train weighed 85 tons, including 13.5 tons of batteries. Its passenger capacity was 140 divided into first and third class compartments.

The first Drumm train, Railcar A, was completed early in 1932 and introduced to daily service on the Amiens Street-Bray coastal line where it made a number of round trips, with a recharge of its batteries taking place between trips from charging equipment installed at each end. A second identical train, Railcar B, entered service on the Harcourt Street Line in October 1932. It was provided with charging facilities at Harcourt Street by the Dublin United Tramway Company, which had an electricity sub-station for its electric trams at Hatch Street below the station's buffer stops. The new Drumm train was highly popular on the Harcourt Street Line, although its commercial viability was disputed by leading consulting engineers who believed that a more lightweight railcar design was needed. By all accounts Railcars A and B were extremely reliable and virtually accident free.

Their reliability and popularity encouraged the construction of two further Drumm trains during 1938 of a more modern and lighter design. They were Railcars C and D, both of which entered service on the Harcourt Street Line late in 1939. They were soon joined by Railcars A and B, so that by 1940 four two-coach Drumm trains were operating the bulk of the Harcourt Street-Bray service. This would seem to indicate that passenger traffic on the line even in those days was relatively light. During the 'Emergency' years of the Second World War, when coal shortages severely curtailed steam trains, the Drumm trains became the mainstay of the Harcourt Street Line. They were greatly appreciated by commuters at a time when private car and public bus transport was severely limited by petrol shortages. At the height of the 'Emergency' in 1941, the government ordered that the Drumm trains should cease to operate between 10am and 4pm on weekdays and all day on Sundays in order to conserve electricity.

Dick Flynn, who travelled frequently on the Drumm trains, says that from a passenger's point of view they were comfortable, bright, well lit at night, warm and were silent running. In speaking to The Blackrock Society in 1996 he compared the Drumm trains to other suburban trains as follows:

Drumm trains at Bray: More modern train D, built in 1939, contrasts with the earlier train at rear built in 1932. Both have under-coach batteries visible.

Drumm train B being recharged at Harcourt Street beside Engine No. 436

In the 1930s and '40s most of the suburban passenger stock was comprised of passenger vehicles surplus to the several railways that had been amalgamated into the GSR. There were old 1882 six-wheelers from the GSWR and the MGWR. Many were gas-lit and all six-wheelers were noisy. Compared with these the Drumms were luxury trains. The Drumm trains had a unique sound as the power bogies had a heavier 'dum dum' than that of the leading and trailing bogies. The motors sounded much like the DART of today, especially when reversed to slow down the train, or on the hilly descents of the Harcourt Street Line when the current regenerated helped recharge the batteries. The Drumm trains never developed wheel 'flats' like the DART or the six-wheelers. The open-plan seating made finding friends easy as compared with compartment stock.

The suburban rail system of the 1930s and '40s and indeed later was very much a community system. The staff knew the passengers and the passengers knew one another, and the Drumm cars with their open saloons enhanced this community spirit. The cars had a fairly commodious van compartment where luggage, prams and bicycles were carried.

When CIÉ was formed in 1945 to take over the railways from the GSR, a study made of the operating costs per passenger seat of the Drumm trains revealed that they were nearly four times that of steam trains on suburban routes. These figures did not augur well for the Drumm trains, but they continued to operate on the Harcourt Street Line until 1949 when the batteries had reached the end of their working life. As CIÉ was incurring a rising annual deficit and was under government pressure at that time to reduce costs, the decision was taken to end the use of the Drumm trains and not to incur further expenditure on them. The last Drumm battery-operated train left Bray for a return trip to Harcourt Street on 12 July 1949, two days after the last cars operated on

Mixed Trains

Up until 1950, the Harcourt Street Line was unique in the Dublin area for having what were known as 'mixed trains' usually seen only on rural branch lines. These trains consisted both of passenger and goods vehicles and would shunt at intermediate stations to pick up or set down goods wagons, while the bemused passengers were being shaken about in their own compartments. As the goods sidings at the intermediate stations of Shankill, Foxrock and Dundrum on the Harcourt Street Line all faced towards Dublin, most of the shunting took place on the daily mid-afternoon 'mixed' from Bray. Goods wagons were attached or detached as required and the train was allowed an extra 15 minutes in the timetable for the shunting operations involved. The wagons were brought to Harcourt Street and assembled there for return to Bray the following day on the mid-morning 'mixed' which was allowed an extra 5 minutes because of its slower speed.

Dick Flynn recalls that the Harcourt Street Line had a light goods traffic and that the 3.20pm was the daily 'mixed train' from Bray. It collected and delivered wagons, vans and horse boxes from the intermediate stations and was quite often worked by a single Drumm train unit, which arrived in Harcourt Street with a small goods train in tow. Regular goods traffic included agricultural produce from Shankill, beet wagons and horse boxes from Foxrock and covered wagons for the Pye Ireland factory in Dundrum. The goods traffic was taken to Bray on the 11am 'mixed' and forwarded from there to its ultimate destination. Dick Flynn recalls that complicated shunting operations were often involved at the intermediate stations, especially in Foxrock where the unfortunate passengers had to endure the shunting needed to reach wagons stored on its many sidings.

the Dublin electric tram system to Blackrock (Route No.6), Dún Laoghaire (No.7) and Dalkey (No. 8).

Following termination of the Drumm trains, the batteries and electrical control equipment were removed from all four trains and the railcars were converted to ordinary passenger carriages. These were used on steam-hauled passenger trains on the Harcourt Street Line, notably the 8.50am 'Express' from Bray, until diesel railcars replaced these trains in 1955. Subsequently the old Drumm trains were stored on a siding at Foxrock awaiting scrapping. Railcars A and B were scrapped in 1956/7, but the more modern Railcars C and D remained stored at Foxrock until the closure and abandonment of the Harcourt Street Line. They survived until 1964 when they were finally scrapped. This ended the era of the Drumm trains, the earliest electric operation of suburban trains in Dublin. Unlike the much later DART and Luas imported from abroad, the Drumm trains were uniquely an Irish invention fully and very successfully realised in Ireland by Irish scientists, engineers and craftsmen.

CHAPTER 10

Accidents

· · · · · · · · · · · · · · · · · ·

THE HARCOURT STREET ACCIDENT 1900

One of the most spectacular accidents in Irish railway history happened at Harcourt Street Station on St Valentine's Day 1900. An incoming cattle train from Enniscorthy failed to stop, crashed through the buffer stops and the outer station wall, leaving the engine perched precariously above Hatch Street some nine metres below. Miraculously nobody was killed but the driver of the train was trapped in the wreckage and had to have his right arm amputated.

The train, hauled by 0-6-0 locomotive 17 'Wicklow', had left Enniscorthy at 10am that morning with a load of 29 cattle wagons preceded by a timber wagon and with a guard's van at the rear. It stopped at Gorey and Arklow to load cattle from a fair and its final stop was at Foxrock, where one wagon was detached. On leaving Foxrock the train climbed steadily to the summit of the Harcourt Street Line at Lakelands beyond Stillorgan, where steam was shut off and the train rolled down the gradient through Dundrum and Milltown towards Harcourt Street Station. Only as the train was crossing the Grand Canal Bridge, where the rails were described at the subsequent inquiry as being 'very greasy', did the driver realise that the handbrake fully applied to the coal tender's wheels would not be sufficient to stop the train at the terminus. The driver applied the vacuum brake, then put the engine into reverse gear and finally turned on full steam but to no avail, as with the momentum generated by its heavy load the train could not stop. It continued through the station at a rapidly reducing speed, but crashed the buffer stops and ploughed through the metre-thick outer wall of the station.

Fortunately neither the fireman, guard, cattlemen, their beasts nor anyone on the street below were injured. The fireman had jumped clear just before the impact, but the 22-year old driver, William Hyland, who remained at his post was trapped by his right arm between the engine and its coal tender. The tender had fallen backwards from the

outer wall into the pit separating it from the buffer stops, where it lay on its end together with the leading timber wagon. Before the unfortunate driver could be extricated from the wreckage, his right arm had to be amputated below the shoulder. The following day a twenty-ton crane lowered the engine down to street level at the top of Hatch Street. There a temporary track was laid along the street to Earlsfort Terrace and into Adelaide

View of crashed engine perched precariously above Hatch Street

Bridge over the Grand Canal in the 1950s

Road as far as the ramp that led up to the goods yard at the eastern side of Harcourt Street station.

A subsequent Board of Trade (BOT) inquiry into the cause of the accident found that the driver must have entirely misjudged his speed on entering the station. The handbrake only should have been used and clearly the buffer stops were wanting in strength. The BOT report added that if means could be found to dispense with the turntable at the end of the line, it would be possible to bring forward the buffer stops and lessen the risks of future accidents. However the railway company of the time, the Dublin Wicklow & Wexford Railway (DW&WR), decided not to disturb the turntable, which remained a most unusual feature of the terminus until its final closure in 1958. The suggested strengthening of the buffer stops was implemented and a very strong monolithic concrete bastion to the stops was built. This proved its worth as it prevented the recurrence of similar accidents after 1900.

The most significant consequence of this 1900 accident was the introduction by the DW&WR of a new regulation specifying a mandatory stop for all incoming trains at Ranelagh to ensure that they would approach Harcourt Street station at a moderate speed in future. That regulation remained in force until the closure of the Harcourt Street Line at the end of 1958.

In more recent years an explanation for the spectacular Harcourt Street accident has been advanced. It has been recorded that in the days of steam trains many of the older drivers were careful to blow the engine's whistle before crossing the Grand Canal Bridge. When asked the reason, their answer was 'to warn the fairies'. Many found this amusing and regarded it merely as an old superstitious custom. However, according to the late historian Deirdre Kelly in her book *Four Roads to Dublin*, a map of Dublin by John Rocque in 1757 shows a 'Fairy Rath' at the point where the railway crossed the Grand Canal. This rath was destroyed in the building of the Grand Canal and the fairies were obliged thereafter to reside underneath the canal at that point. The older drivers on the Harcourt Street Line were aware of this and always blew the whistle to warn the fairies of a train's approach. Unfortunately, on St Valentine's Day 1900, the driver of the ill-fated cattle train was so preoccupied with trying to stop his train that he forgot to give the fairies their customary warning – with disastrous results!

THE DUNDRUM ACCIDENT 1957

The closing days of 1957 were marred by an unfortunate collision between two diesel railcar trains in the deep rock cutting south of Dundrum station. The trains involved were the 5.20pm Bray-Harcourt Street, comprising a railcar set with an intermediate coach, and the 5.40pm Bray-Harcourt Street of similar composition.

The accident occurred in darkness around 6pm on 23 December about a half-mile on the Bray side of Dundrum station. The circumstances, as described in the subsequent inquiry, give an unusual insight into the working of the Harcourt Street Line in its latter days. A CIÉ employee alighting from a Dublin train at Stillorgan station told the boy porter that there was a cow on the line near Dundrum. The porter telephoned Foxrock station and told the foreman, who sent his boy porter to tell the signalman. He in turn informed the signalman at Dundrum by telephone that there was a cow somewhere on the line between Stillorgan and Dundrum. On receiving this message around 5.30pm the signalman left his cabin in order to instruct the permanent way ganger to go out on the line and remove the animal. The ganger collected his oil lamp, lit it and walked along the track towards Stillorgan.

At a distance of about a half-mile south of Dundrum he met the 5.20pm from Bray, which was moving very slowly with the cow in front of it. This was around 5.55pm but the animal could not be driven off to the side of the line because, at this point, the line was in a deep rock cutting. So the ganger proceeded to drive the cow in front of the slow-moving train in the direction of Dundrum for about 500 yards when, suddenly, the train was violently struck in the rear by the 5.40pm from Bray. Apparently the red tail lamp fixed to the rear of the 5.20pm train had extinguished, because its oil container

Crashed diesel railcars near Dundrum

had not been refilled at Bray. Had it been showing red, it is possible that the 5.40pm could have stopped before the collision.

The first of the two trains had left Bray nine minutes late due to difficulty in fuelling the heating system of the railcar. The train called at all stations to Foxrock, where neither the guard nor the driver was warned of the cow on the line ahead. The train stopped briefly at Stillorgan but here both the driver and guard were warned by the boy porter. The driver treated the message as a caution and proceeded slowly towards Dundrum. Over half a mile from Dundrum he saw the animal and slowed down to walking pace, driving the cow in front. The second train had left Bray on time and left Foxrock around 5.55pm without receiving any warning of possible danger. Leaving Stillorgan the train ran 'at a fast rate of about 45-50 miles per hour' and only had begun to apply the normal braking on the descent to Dundrum when the violent collision occurred.

The leading railcar of the second train crashed into the rear railcar of the first train and over-rode it for nearly a coach length, displacing the rear bogie of the first train and causing severe damage to both railcars. The cab and leading first-class compartment of the second train were completely devastated and the unfortunate driver, Andy Larkin of Bray, was killed instantly. The guard of the first train and three out of a total of twenty passengers on both trains were injured. They were taken to hospital, but all were soon discharged.

Immediately after the collision, all traffic on the Harcourt Street Line was brought to a standstill. An alternative bus service calling at all stations by an extremely circuitous route was substituted, but full train services were not restored until after Christmas.

Train from Harcourt Street at Milltown in 1951

Outline History of the Harcourt Street Line

· ·

During the railway-building mania of the 1840s, three separate companies sought powers from the Westminster parliament to build a railway from Dublin to Bray. The Dublin & Kingstown Railway, Ireland's first railway which opened in 1834, sought to extend their line along the coast from Kingstown (now Dún Laoghaire) to Bray. The Great Western Railway in England, anxious to establish a footing in Ireland, promoted the Waterford, Wexford, Wicklow & Dublin Railway to follow an inland route from Bray to Dublin. A third company, the Dublin, Dundrum & Enniskerry Railway was persuaded by parliament to restrict their line to Dundrum, with a branch from Ranelagh to Rathfarnham, and to become known as the Dublin, Dundrum & Rathfarnham Railway. On 16 July 1846 three separate bills empowering these companies to build their railways received the Royal Assent, thereby giving birth to the Harcourt Street Line. Highlights from the line's subsequent history are set out beneath.

1849	Contract to build the Dublin, Dundrum & Rathfarnham Railway awarded to William Dargan, who began work near Churchtown in April.
1851	Two further bills received Royal Assent. Certain powers of WWW&DR repealed and company's name changed to Dublin & Wicklow Railway. Also certain powers of DD&RR repealed and name changed to Dublin & Bray Railway. Contracts for both railways awarded to William Dargan.
1853	Dublin & Wicklow Railway completed line from Bray to Dundrum. As the Dublin & Bray Railway had failed to complete their line from Dublin to Dundrum, they were taken over by the D&WR.

1854	Single-line railway opened to public traffic on 10 July from a temporary terminus at Harcourt Road to Bray, with four intermediate stations at Dundrum, Stillorgan, Carrickmines and Shankill.
1855	Doubling of track from Bray to Shanganagh Junction, where coastal line from Westland Row and Kingstown joined the Harcourt Street Line.
1857	Decision to build terminus at Harcourt Street and abandon earlier plans to extend closer to city centre at St Stephen's Green.
1858	First accident on 26 March when train from Wicklow collided with carriages at platform in Harcourt Road, injuring three passengers. First excursion trains advertised for Wicklow Races.
1859	Harcourt Street station opened on 7 February. Temporary platform built at Foxrock on site of planned station at new housing development.
1860	New station opened at Milltown. To improve services, line doubled as far as Dundrum. To reflect ambitions, D&WR changed its name to the Dublin, Wicklow & Wexford Railway.
1861	Dundrum to Shanganagh Junction section doubled to create continuous double-track railway from Harcourt Street to Bray. New station opened in Foxrock at request of Mr Bentley, a developer.
1862	Siding provided at Shankill for ore trafffic to Ballycorus lead-works.
1872	Boiler of locomotive exploded at Bray, killing driver and fireman.
1873	Additional sidings and goods stores built at Harcourt Street station.
1876	Level crossing and siding built at Foxrock at request of Rev Sullivan.
1877	Shanganagh Junction dispensed with following provision of a separate track from Kingstown to Bray parallel to the two Harcourt Street tracks.
1885	To facilitate crossing the railway, footbridges erected at Dundrum and Stillorgan stations.
1888	In connection with a proposed racecourse at Leopardstown, a Captain Quinn requested additional passenger accommodation and sidings at

Foxrock. A third platform, connected with existing platforms by a long footbridge, was built as well as extra sidings for horse traffic.

1890   Collision at Shankill between the Wexford train and a Bray goods train, injuring one passenger.

1891   Light engine collided at Leopardstown with horse and cart, killing its driver.

1894   Signal cabin at Foxrock blown down in storm, injuring the signalman.

1896   Station opened at Rathmines and Ranelagh to compete with expanding services of the Dublin United Tramway Company.

1897   'Wexford Mail' trains from Harcourt Street changed to depart from Westland Row and follow coastal, rather than inland, route to Bray.

1900   Cattle special from Enniscorthy failed to stop in Harcourt Street and ran through end-wall of station, injuring driver.

1907   DW&WR changed its name from 1 January to the Dublin & South Eastern Railway. Private horsebox, painted in owner's colours of dark blue, built for the legendary racehorse owner 'Boss' Croker and kept in special shed at Foxrock. On the occasion of visit of King Edward VII to Leopardstown Races, the level crossing was decorated by the local residents with a triumphal arch.

1908   First train catering services provided from Harcourt Street on through trains to and from Rosslare.

1910   Woodbrook Halt opened to serve cricket ground adjacent to line on the estate of Sir Stanley Cochrane.

1912   Special trains to Foxrock for air race starting from Leopardstown. Derailment of Race Special arriving at Foxrock, injuring one passenger.

1914   Special trains to Woodbrook for air display on the Cochrane Estate.

1915   Due to coastal erosion, line from Kingstown diverted inland between Killiney and Bray. As part of this diversion, Shanganagh Junction was restored to connect the Harcourt Street with the other double-track line.

Foxrock Signalman
Vincent Hanney, 1953

1916	In Easter Rising on 24 April, Harcourt Street station seized by rebels and occupied for two days causing suspension of train services.
1917	Engine ran through engine shed at Harcourt Street and fell into garden.
1920	Woodbrook Golf Club instituted on the Cochrane Estate and decided to retain Woodbrook Halt for golfers until its closure in 1960.
1921	During War of Independence, armed raid on Milltown station.
1922	During Civil War, two road bridges at Shankill blown up and attempt made to blow up Loughlinstown Viaduct. Foxrock signal cabin was

burnt to the ground. Experimental 'omnibus' train of engine, one coach and small van was introduced as an economy measure on Sundays with tickets issued by a conductor/guard, instead of by staff at stations.

1923   Early morning mail train raided at Carrickmines and mailbags taken. Two carriages destroyed by fire at Foxrock and temporary signal cabin first burnt and later blown up. Varying degrees of damage caused to signal cabins at Dundrum, Shankill and Shanganagh Junction.

1925   In accordance with the Railways Act 1924, the Great Southern Railway absorbed D&SER from 1 January 1925. In subsequent rationalisation, Harcourt Street goods depot was closed and goods for the South-East were henceforth handled by North Wall MGW depot.

1927   Major rebuilding of Bray station with a second platform provided on seaward side, mainly for the use of Harcourt Street Line trains.

1929   Clayton steam railcars operated for short period from Harcourt Street to Foxrock. Discontinued due to poor steaming and high coal usage.

1932   First Drumm battery train introduced on Harcourt Street-Bray service.

1938   Electric colour-light signals installed from Harcourt Street to Ranelagh.

1939   Further Drumm battery trains introduced and soon most services on the line were operated by two-coach electric Drumm trains.

1949   Drumm trains discontinued when batteries reached end of working life.

1954   Diesel railcars introduced on some Harcourt Street-Bray services.

1956   Only two steam trains daily in each direction on line, compared with twenty diesel railcar workings. Diesel locomotives replaced steam on Rosslare mainline trains and on the 'Sea Breeze' excursions.

1957   Closure of Bray engine shed on 24 June, ending steam operation on the line. Collision of two diesel railcar trains near Dundrum, killing driver of one train and injuring guard of the other and three passengers.

1958   Closure of Harcourt Street-Shanganagh Junction line on 31 December.

1959	Abandonment Order made within three months of closure. Overbridges removed from Harcourt Road as far as Dundrum to discourage any agitation for reopening the line.
1960	Dismantling of line finally completed by September. Salvaged track exported to India. All property diposed of by public auction realising a total of £150,000.
1970	CIÉ Annual Report revealed 14% increase on previous year in suburban rail travel, due to growing road traffic congestion in the Dublin area.
1972	Dublin County Council and Dublin Corporation adopted the County Dublin Development Plan that retained the trackbed of the former Harcourt Street Line as a public transport reservation free of future development and planning permissions.
1973	CIÉ commissioned a study of a Rapid Rail Transport System for Dublin that included a busway from the city to Dundrum along the Harcourt Street Line trackbed.
1979	Government approved first step of proposed Rapid Transit System by authorising the electrification of the Howth-Bray railway, but excluding the former Harcourt Street Line.
1984	DART electric suburban trains began on Howth-Bray line on 23 July.
1994	Following the Dublin Transportation Initiative Report, the government requested CIÉ to begin preliminary planning of three light rail transit (LRT) routes to link city centre with Tallaght, Ballymun and Cabinteely.
1997	In May CIÉ applied for Light Railway Order (LRO) for Tallaght-Balally via city centre line and government approved funding for this LRT line and its extension to Sandyford. After general election in June, government decided to delay progress pending investigation of underground option in city centre.
1998	Consultants recommended surface system as the most appropriate and cost-effective option. This was not favoured by government who decided to terminate Sandyford LRT line at St Stephen's Green and run underground from there to Broadstone, Ballymun and Dublin Airport.

Former Harcourt Street train drivers, Jim Kiernan and Seán Ó Cinnéide, at Sandyford after their first trip on the Luas Green Line.

LRT system to be designated in future as Luas.

1999   CIÉ withdrew earlier application for LRO and applied for two LROs for the separate Luas lines to Sandyford and Tallaght. Minister for Transport finally approved LRO for Luas Line B to Sandyford in September.

2000   CIÉ began preliminary clearance work along trackbed of old Harcourt Street LIne.

2001   In June work began on major cable-stayed bridge for Luas over wide road junction at Dundrum. In December the Railway Procurement Agency (RPA) was established under new legislation to subsume role of former CIÉ Light Rail Project Office.

2002   Work began on building new bridges over roads and the Grand Canal at the exact same locations as the old Harcourt Street Line bridges demolished in 1959. First tracks laid on the old railway formation between Stillorgan and Balally in September. Major Luas bridge at Dundrum completed in October.

2003   First tram for Luas Line B delivered to Sandyford depot in February. Test running from April between Sandyford and Balally. Rock cutting south of Dundrum widened for possible future use as part of planned Dublin Metro.

2004   New line designated Luas Green Line. Energised from Sandyford to Dundrum in February and to St Stephen's Green in March. Testing over full line began in April. Green Line officially opened on 30 June, carrying 440,000 passengers during first five days of free travel. Minister for Transport announced on 1 November the possibility of providing a centre-city connection from Luas Green Line terminus at St Stephen's Green to the Luas Red Line at O'Connell Street within two years.

Appendices

. . . .

1. Gradient Profile of the Harcourt Street Line

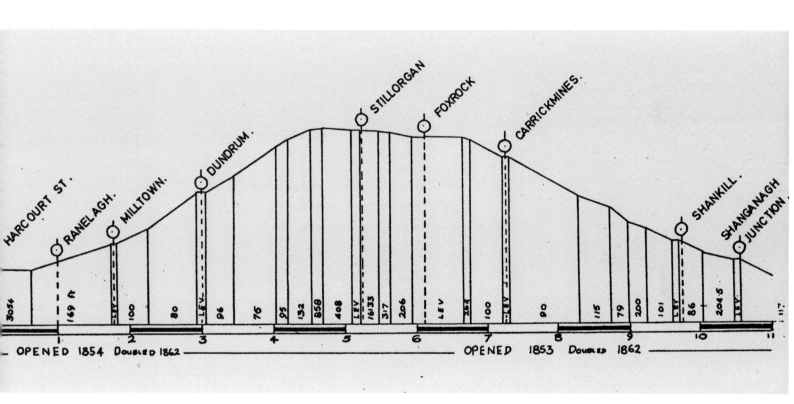

2. Harcourt Street Line timetable for 26 December 1953

26th December, 1953.

DOWN TRAINS — HARCOURT STREET LINE

	a.m.	a.m.	a.m.	a.m.	a.m.	p.m.	p.m.	p.m.	p.m.	p.m.	p.m.	p.m.	p.m.	p.m.	p.m.	p.m.	p.m.	p.m.	p.m.	p.m.
Harcourt Street dep.	8 40	9 40	11 20	11 40	11 55	12 15	12 30	1 35	3 30	4 10	4 20	4 40	4 55	5 30	6 05	7 05	8 45	10 10	11 10	
Ranelagh	8 44	9 44	Non-Stop	Non-Stop	11 59	Non-Stop	Non-Stop	1 39	3 34	Non-Stop	Non-Stop	4 44	Empty Non-Stop	5 34	6 09	7 09	8 49	10 14	11 14	
Milltown	8 47	9 47			p.m. 12 03			1 42	3 38			4 47		5 37	6 12	7 12	8 52	10 17	11 17	
Dundrum	8 52	9 52			12 09			1 47	3 44			4 52		5 42	6 17	7 17	8 57	10 22	11 22	
Stillorgan	8 58	9 58			12 16			1 53	3 51			4 58		5 48	6 23	7 23	9 03	10 28	11 28	
Foxrock		10 01	11 37	11 57	12 19	12 32	12 47	1 56	4 00	4 27	4 37	5 01	5 12	5 51	6 26	7 26	9 06	10 31	11 31	
Carrickmines		10 04			12 22			1 59	4 04			5 04		5 54	6 29	7 29	9 09	10 34	11 34	
Shankill		10 09			12 27			2 04	4 09			5 09		5 59	6 34	7 34	9 14	10 39	11 39	
Bray arr.		10 15			12 33			2 10	4 15			5 15		6 05	6 40	7 40	9 20	10 45	11 45	
Bray dep.	7 00	10 22						2 23	4 20						6 40	7 48	9 28		a.m. 11 54	
Greystones arr.	7 12	10 34						2 35	4 32						7 13	8 00	9 40		a.m. 12 06	

KINGSBRIDGE.

26th December, 1953.

UP TRAINS — HARCOURT STREET LINE

	a.m.	a.m.	a.m.	a.m.	a.m.	p.m.	p.m.	p.m.	p.m.	p.m.	p.m.	p.m.	p.m.	p.m.	p.m.	p.m.	p.m.	p.m.	p.m.	p.m.	a.m.
Greystones dep.	7 30	7 42			11 40	11 52	2 20	2 30	3 50	4 00	4 55	5 07	6 21	6 33		8 20	8 32	10 00	10 12		12 20
Bray arr.						Noon 12 00	2 27														12 32
Bray dep.	7 50	7 57	9 25	11 10		p.m. 12 07	2 30		4 02	4 05	5 10	5 17	5 23	6 27	6 50	6 57	7 03	8 40	8 47	10 20	
Shankill	7 57		9 32	11 17		12 13	Non-Stop		Non-Stop		5 17	5 23			6 57	7 03		8 47	8 53	10 27	
Carrickmines	8 03		9 38	11 23		12 17				4 15	5 23	5 27			7 03	7 07		8 53	8 57	10 33	
Foxrock	8 07		9 42	11 27	11 12	12 17	2 37			4 30	5 27	5 30			7 07	7 10		8 57	9 00	10 37	
Stillorgan	8 10		9 45	11 30		12 20	2 40		4 12	4 33	5 30	5 36			7 10	7 16		9 00	9 06	10 40	
Dundrum	8 16		9 51	11 36		12 26	2 46			4 39	5 36	5 39			7 16	7 19		9 06	9 09	10 46	
Milltown	8 19		9 54	11 39		12 29	2 49		4 14	4 44	5 39	5 42			7 19	7 22		9 09	9 12	10 49	
Ranelagh	8 22		9 57	11 42		12 32	2 52	Non-Stop	4 27	4 47	5 42	5 45			7 22	7 25		9 12	9 15	10 52	
Harcourt Street arr.	8 25		10 00	11 45	11 30	12 35	2 55	4 05	4 15	4 30	4 50	5 00	5 20	5 45	6 55	7 25		9 15		10 55	

(To Westland Row.)

BY ORDER.

3. Map of Harcourt Street Line

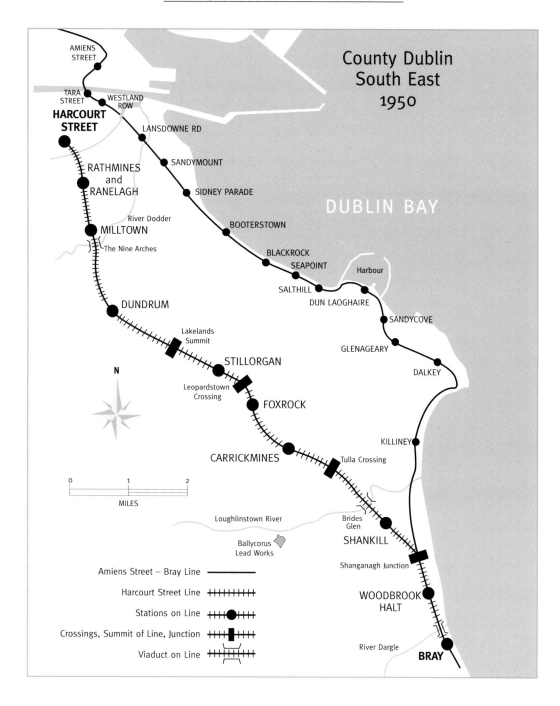

County Dublin
South East
1950

DUBLIN BAY

AMIENS STREET

TARA STREET
WESTLAND ROW

HARCOURT STREET

LANSDOWNE RD

SANDYMOUNT

RATHMINES and RANELAGH

SIDNEY PARADE

River Dodder

BOOTERSTOWN

MILLTOWN

The Nine Arches

BLACKROCK

SEAPOINT

Harbour

SALTHILL

DUNDRUM

DUN LAOGHAIRE

SANDYCOVE

Lakelands Summit

GLENAGEARY

STILLORGAN

DALKEY

N

Leopardstown Crossing

FOXROCK

KILLINEY

CARRICKMINES

Tulla Crossing

0   1   2
MILES

Loughlinstown River

Brides Glen

Ballycorus Lead Works

SHANKILL

Shanganagh Junction

Amiens Street – Bray Line
Harcourt Street Line
Stations on Line
Crossings, Summit of Line, Junction
Viaduct on Line

WOODBROOK HALT

River Dargle

BRAY

4. Text of 'Withdrawal of Services'

THE Board of C.I.E. are aware that a certain amount of inconvenience will be caused to members of the public who have habitually used the Harcourt Street/Bray line, following the decision to withdraw passenger services from this Section. The Board know that many have used the line over the years and it will be an upset to their travelling habits. The Board feel that these regular travellers should be fully informed as to the reasons which compel the closing of the line and should be informed of the alternative services which will be provided by buses, and that it is intended to give an equally good service by road and so cause the minimum of inconvenience.

THE facts are that, under the recent Transport Act, C.I.E. is obliged within five years to be financially self-supporting and, to this end, it must effect radical economies. The first and most obvious economy is to abandon services which are unremunerative and which show no possibility of being made remunerative. Unfortunately the Harcourt Street/Bray line is in this category. The annual loss, that is the excess of expenditure over revenue, from the provision of services on this line is £53,000, and the estimated annual saving which will accrue to the Board from the withdrawal of services, and after providing for the cost of substitute services, will be £47,000.

As the result of the withdrawal of rail equipment from the Harcourt Street/Bray Section the Board will save a further £24,000 by the use of this equipment on other sections, particularly under the head of substitution of Diesel Rail Cars for steam worked locomotives, so that the effect of the withdrawal of the rail services from the Harcourt Street/Bray line will be a reduction in the present deficit by £71,000 per annum.

IN view of these facts, it is hoped that the users of the service will understand that it would be impossible under the new conditions created by the recent Transport Act to continue to operate rail services on the Harcourt Street/Bray line.

THE existing bus services, mentioned overleaf, cover the territory served by rail between Harcourt Street and Bray, and an additional service is being introduced between Bray and Dublin via Dundrum. It will be remembered, of course, that the railway service on the Westland Row line will remain for the use of through passengers between Dublin and Bray who hitherto have enjoyed the facility of a terminal at Harcourt Street.

FRANK LEMASS,
General Manager.

Córas Iompair Éireann,
Kingsbridge Station,
Dublin.
29th October, 1958.

5. Advertisements re New Travel Arrangements in 1959

AUCTIONS

Daniel Morrissey & Sons
LTD.

IMPORTANT
PRELIMINARY NOTICE

ON THE INSTRUCTIONS OF CORAS IOMPAIR
EIREANN, WE WILL OFFER

FOR SALE
By Public Auction

ON A DATE TO BE ANNOUNCED LATER

HARCOURT STREET
STATION BUILDINGS

Bounded by Harcourt Street, Hatch Street, Harcourt Road
and Adelaide Road.

The property will be offered for sale in six lots as
follows:—

LOT 1
The extensive building and ground leased to Irish Dunlop
Company, Limited, for ten years from 1953 at £1,600 per
annum, tenant paying rates.

LOT 2
The large modern factory premises at Adelaide Road leased
to Auto Services, Limited, for twenty-one years from 1949
at £400 per annum, tenant paying rates.

LOT 3
The large garage and filling station at the corner of
Harcourt Street and Harcourt Road leased to Auto Services,
Limited, for ninety-nine year from 1945 at £255 per annum,
tenant paying rates.

LOT 4
Modern building at Hatch Street leased to Wilson & Company, Limited, for ninety-nine years from 1957 at £156 per
annum, tenant paying rates.

LOT 5
The very extensive vaults at Harcourt Street leased to W. &
A. Gilbey, Limited, for forty-two years from 1926 at £1,000
per annum, tenant paying rates.

LOT 6
THE ENTIRE STATION PREMISES
INCLUDING THE VERY IMPOSING AND
VALUABLE FRONTAGE TO HARCOURT
STREET; MAIN ENTRANCE HALL; BOOKING
OFFICES; REFRESHMENT ROOM, etc.;
COVERED PLATFORMS; PERMANENT WAY
AND A LARGE AREA OF UNCOVERED
GROUND.
ENTRANCES FROM HARCOURT STREET AND
ADELAIDE ROAD.

COMPLETE VACANT POSSESSION
OF THIS LOT

FULL PARTICULARS LATER.
SOLICITOR: BRENDAN McGRATH, ESQ., ST. JOHN'S,
ISLANDBRIDGE, INCHICORE.

Daniel Morrissey & Sons
LTD.

AUCTIONEERS AND VALUERS, M.I.A.A.
LOWER MERRION STREET, DUBLIN
Telephone: 65781—5 lines.

7. DLRCC Notice of Proposed New Railway to Cherrywood

**Extension of LUAS Line B1
Sandyford to Cherrywood**

**Planning and Development Act 2000
(Section 49)**

**Supplementary Development
Contribution Scheme**

*Extension of LUAS Line B1
Sandyford to Cherrywood*

Notice is hereby given pursuant to Section 49 of the Planning and Development Act, 2000 that on 13th January 2003, the Council of the County of Dun Laoghaire-Rathdown made a Supplementary Development Contribution Scheme for the purpose of part financing the extension of the LUAS Line B1 from Sandyford LUAS depot (under construction) to Cherrywood. Developments coming within the catchment area of the adopted scheme will be subject to a supplementary development contribution levy at the rates of:-

Residential: Contribution Rate of €250,000 per gross site hectare

Commercial: Contribution Rate of €570,000 per gross site hectare

Details of the Scheme (including Map) may be inspected at the following locations:

Economic Development & Planning Department
Council Offices
County Hall
Marine Road
Dun Laoghaire
Co. Dublin
(10.00 to 16.00)

Council Offices
Dundrum Office Park
Dundrum
Dublin 14
(09.30 to 12.30 and 13.30 to 16.30)

Details of the Scheme (including Map) may be purchased at the County Council offices at a charge of €5

Details of the Scheme (excluding Map) may be viewed on the County Council website: **www.dlrcoco.ie**

**M. Gough, Director of Services,
Economic Development and Planning Department.**

20th January 2003.

**DUN LAOGHAIRE-RATHDOWN
COUNTY COUNCIL**

Ó Chuan go Sliabh

Comhairle Chontae Dhún Laoghaire - Ráth an Dúin

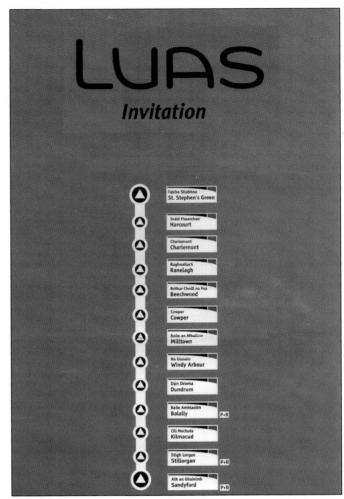